I0161820

CHILDREN
HEARING GOD'S VOICE

PARENT/TEACHER TRAINING GUIDE

ZOE
ZOE Ministries International

Rev. 05/2019

PHOTOCOPYING AND DISTRIBUTION POLICY

The content in this Parent/Teacher Training Guide is copyrighted material owned by ZOE Ministries International. Please do not reproduce content in emails or on websites.

For families: You may make as many photocopies of the Workbook pages as you need for use WITHIN YOUR OWN FAMILY ONLY. DO NOT MAKE PHOTOCOPIES OF THIS PARENT/TEACHER GUIDE. Photocopying the pages so that the Workbook can then be resold is a violation of copyright.

Schools and Co-ops MAY NOT PHOTOCOPY any portion of the Parent/Teacher Training Guide. The best option is to purchase a Guide for each teacher.

For ordering, go to our website www.zoeministries.org or call 303-673-9658.

CONTENTS

Dear Parent/Teacher,

We are excited that you have decided to train children to hear, recognize and follow God's voice! *Children Hearing God's Voice* is an exciting, hands-on course for five to ten-year olds that has been adapted from the adult curriculum.

As we examine the Scripture **John 10:27**, "My sheep hear my voice, and I know them, and they follow me (NKJV)," we realize that when Jesus was saying this, He may not have been directing it only to His disciples. There were probably children within earshot of His voice. We believe the Lord wants to, and does, speak to His children of *all* ages.

Jesus said in **John 14:11-12**, "Believe me when I say that I am in the Father and the Father is in me; or at least believe on the evidence of the miracles themselves. I tell you the truth, anyone who has faith in me will do what I have been doing. He will do even greater things than these, because I am going to the Father."

Children are open to the work of the Lord, and they need to be equipped to continue Jesus' ministry. Learning to listen to God's voice will enable children to go forth to preach the kingdom of God, heal the sick, and minister where the Lord leads. We live in exciting times, and we all need to be prepared to do kingdom work.

It is our prayer that the Holy Spirit will unlock hearts to better understand and recognize God's voice. May the Lord bless you as He reveals His desire to be in deeper relationship with *all* of His children.

In His Service,
Dick and Ginny Chanda

INTRODUCTION FOR PARENTS/TEACHERS

We want to share some key information with you before you jump into this training course with your children.

1. This course will help you train children to listen more attentively and to recognize what God is saying to them. We expect that you will be learning how to hear God's voice more clearly right along with the children. Do not be intimidated. God wants to speak to us even more than we want to hear Him.

2. If this material is used by a small family, you may want to invite another family to go through the course with you. The more the merrier! It is helpful to see how God speaks to other people. However, that family should buy their own set of materials.

3. You can go through this course again and again with the children at different stages of development. We learn best by repetition, do we not? The learning activities and art projects included in the lessons cover a wide range of abilities between the ages of five and ten. What a child doesn't do now can be done at a later stage.

4. Some of the activities in the Workbook involve writing. We have included sets of lines at the back of the Workbook. These can be placed behind a Workbook page to help a child write in a straight line. If you have children who are working on handwriting, go to www.allkidsnetwork.com for free worksheets.

5. If the children are too young to write, feel free to have them dictate to you what they would like written in their Workbook. Successful use of this material in a classroom of young children may depend upon having a sufficient number of adults to help. If your children are not yet adept at reading, you may want to omit having them read the book by Loren Cunningham. Instead, you might share with the children any part that includes a real life instance of hearing from God.

6. During learning activities and art projects, the children will be asked to trace some of the patterns in the back of the Workbook. We recommend that you print those pages on card stock. It will make tracing them easier. If your printer cannot handle card stock, you may want to have them printed at a print shop.

7. When you are directed to find and read aloud a scripture, take the time to help each child find the verses in his Bible. This allows the scriptures to have greater effect in each heart and will increase the children's Bible literacy level. A suggestion is to use adhesive book tabs that can be added to any Bible, helping the children find verses more quickly.

8. If a child has not yet asked Jesus into his life, and he expresses interest, see the "Salvation Scriptures" page at the back of this book. It has some verses you can share with the child and a sample prayer to use to lead him in salvation.

9. Have the children write out and begin memorizing the Key Scripture in their Workbook early in the week. Agree who will be the ministry recipient early in the week as well, giving you and the children time to hear God as to what He wants you all to share with that person.

10. You may choose to divide each lesson into portions for each day. For example, you could complete each lesson in four days, dividing the scriptures and activities/projects between those days. Be sure to reserve time for ministry on the last day.

11. Within the Teaching Content section of each lesson, we mention specific Learning Activities (LA) and Art Projects (AP) that reinforce what has just been taught. Descriptions of the activities and projects are listed at the end of each lesson.

12. If you are teaching a wide range of ages, it may be helpful to give related coloring pages to the younger children as you cover higher level material with the older children. Some coloring pages have been included in the Workbook but you can find additional pages by going to www.bing.pinterest/biblecoloringpages. Students of varying ages can view YouTube videos illustrating the Bible accounts that are included in the curriculum.

PRAYER AND MINISTRY TIME

An exciting part of this course is this Prayer and Ministry section where children learn to "hear from God" and then pray for and "minister" to others as He directs them. According to John 10:27, "My sheep hear my voice…." We are His sheep! Because such "ministry" may be new to some, we are providing some rather detailed helps. (In Lesson 2, more extensive Scripture guidance is offered.)

1. This course provides hands-on training to minister to others. You want to create a fun and safe environment for the children in which they can learn to hear from God and minister as He directs. No one hears clearly all the time, so this is a chance to practice. So, each lesson will have a prayer and ministry time after the teaching section.

2. Lesson 1 gives you the opportunity to model what it looks like to minister under the direction of the Lord, as you lay hands on and speak a blessing over each child. In Lessons 2-13, you will be instructed to choose a person who will receive prayer and ministry for that lesson. The children will record this person's name in their Workbook. You should each agree to ask God to tell you something that will encourage that person.

3. At the beginning of each week, starting with Lesson 2, choose one person to receive ministry from you and the children. The designated person could be a sibling, friend, parent, grandparent or other relative, a missionary or neighbor. Agree to pray for that person as you cover the material in the lesson. Ask God to share with each of you something He wants to say to that person. It should always be something that will be encouraging. God will decide how He wants to speak to each of you. He could give you a dream, a Scripture verse, a single word, or a picture in your mind. Encourage everyone to write down what they think God said in the Workbook.

4. It is wonderful to see what God does as we follow His leading during the ministry time. Be sensitive to the Lord's guidance as to when you should minister to the designated person. Have the children share what they heard God say. If the person is not present, the children could share their words of encouragement through any form of communication.

5. In the Workbook, the Prayer and Ministry section is provided for the children to record the name of the person you chose for that lesson. There each child should also record any words of encouragement that the Lord gave him for that person and how he prayed for them. (If a child is not yet writing, he can dictate to you and/or draw a picture.) Beginning in Lesson 2, the children should fill this out for each lesson, recording what God says to them. As God answers the children's prayers, help them record it in their Workbook. This will build up the children's faith.

6. If praying and ministering is a new concept to the children, you should model for the children how to say

what you think God gave you for the ministry recipient. Then pray aloud a simple, short prayer related to what God showed you for the person. Keep your prayer short and sweet! In time, you and the children will be comfortable sharing and praying aloud.

7. When a child gets a word or picture for the designated person, you may need to help him form a prayer related to what God gave him. For example, if a child saw a mental picture of that person with very large, strong legs, you could ask, "What do you think God means by that picture?" If he doesn't know, stop and ask the Lord what it means. God will often give more information. Someone may get a sense that God is saying to stand firm and not be moved from what He has told them is right. Then the prayer could be: "Lord, help them stay strong and not move from what they know is right."

   Or, if a child heard the word "flower," you could ask, "God, what do You want to say about this person and a flower?" Help the child share what he heard. For example, the child might say, "I think God is saying that He sees you as a beautiful flower that He has created." A prayer for that person could be: "Lord, help her see herself the way You see her—as a beautiful flower."

8. ***Share these guidelines for listening to God's voice with the children when you gather for the ministry time, as needed:***

   a. If God gave you something to share with the person, share it during this time. Be sure what you say is encouraging and builds up the person. We don't want to say something that makes them feel bad. If you think you have heard something from God that might not be encouraging or is a word of correction, don't mention it during the ministry time. Instead, share it with your parent/teacher in private. They will give you help to know what God might want to do in this situation.*

      *Parent/Teacher:

      If a child thinks God has communicated something about the ministry recipient that is negative or fearful, and he shares it during the ministry time, say "That's interesting" and move on. Later, lovingly take the child aside. Listen to what they have heard or seen from God. Ask, "What do you think God is saying?" and help them accurately discern God's message. Remember, a word from God will always build up, stir up or comfort (**1 Corinthians 14:3**).

      Here are possible options: 1) God may be asking you both to only pray for the ministry recipient. 2) If action seems needed, you and the child could meet privately with the ministry recipient to share the message. 3) You might want to contact a pastor for further guidance.

   b. If God did not give you anything to share, take time to listen now. Let it be natural. Don't try to make something up.

   c. The way God speaks to you and works in you may be different from how He works in anyone else.

   d. If it seems that everyone but you is hearing God, don't worry. Instead, pray for those He is speaking to.

   e. Let God be God! Let Him speak to you when He wants and how He wants. Give up your ideas of how God will lead you. Relax. He is your Good Shepherd and He wants to speak with you more than you can imagine!

   f. If the person being prayed for is present, say, "Usually, we minister with our eyes open, so that we can see how the person who is being prayed for is doing."

g. In the Bible, sometimes believers placed their hands on a person when they prayed for them. But we should ask the person, "Is it OK for me to place my hand on your shoulder as I pray?" If it is not OK, say, "That's all right. The Lord can work just as well if we pray without laying hands on you." It is important that the person who is receiving ministry is comfortable.

h. As we minister to someone, it is a time for us to practice hearing what God wants to say to the person. Yet, we don't hear clearly all of the time. So, the person who we are praying for should remember this:

*   **If what the person says doesn't make sense, put it on the shelf.**
*   **If what the person says disagrees with what God has told you, let it drop to the ground.**
*   **If the Holy Spirit inside you agrees with what the person says, you should write it down in your Workbook and wait for God to make it happen in the future.**

ADDITIONAL COMMENTS

In this Guide, we use a generic masculine pronoun "him" when referring to a single child. We use this pronoun rather than "he/she" for ease in reading. Like God, we do not favor one gender over another!

LESSON 1

THE BLESSING

OBJECTIVE

Each one of us is valuable to God. He created each of us individually with a special purpose. God blesses us so that we can be a blessing to others.

THE BLESSING

LESSON 1 OBJECTIVE

To understand that each one of us is valuable to God. He created each of us individually with a special purpose. God blesses us so that we can be a blessing to others.

LESSON 1 KEY SCRIPTURE

Each day read aloud this lesson's scripture. Have the children write it out in the Workbook on page 11 in the space provided. Encourage the children to memorize this lesson's verse by the end of the week. Challenge them to recite it without reading it.

Mark 10:14-16 "'Let the little children come to me. Don't keep them away. God's kingdom belongs to people like them. What I'm about to tell you is true. Anyone who will not receive God's kingdom like a little child will never enter it.' And He took the children in His arms, put His hands on them and blessed them."

You may want to shorten the verse for younger children:
Mark 10:14, 16 "'Let the little children come to me...' And He took the children in His arms, put His hands on them and blessed them."

LESSON 1 READING ASSIGNMENT

Chapters 1 and 2 in *Is That Really You, God?*
Some children will need you to read portions of the assigned reading to them, others can read the chapters on their own or take turns reading aloud as a group.

TEACHING CONTENT, LEARNING ACTIVITIES AND ART PROJECTS

These are the largest components of the lesson. Depending upon your children's ages, you will need to decide how much of each section to cover in any given day. Select Learning Activities and Art Projects that fit your children's abilities and interests. Feel free to be creative and have fun as you lead your children into a real relationship with the Lord Jesus.

PRAYER AND MINISTRY TIME

By the end of the week, pray a blessing over each child. Ask the Lord to show you the best way to bless him. You may use any of the sample blessings given in this lesson, but feel free to pray as the Lord leads you. You will be modeling for the children how they will pray for someone else in later lessons, so keep your blessing simple and affirming.

The Blessing

Before teaching this lesson, ask God how He sees each child—his potential, gifts, talents, positive character qualities, as well as areas needing growth. This will be helpful during the prayer and ministry portion of this lesson.

TEACHING CONTENT

A letter to your children

Direct the children to the letter found on the first page of Lesson 1 in the Workbook. Read it aloud to the children, and have them follow along. The text is included below:

Dear children,

Jesus has a special place in His heart for His children of all ages. In the scripture below, He clearly says that the little children should come to Him.

> **"Some people brought little children to Jesus. They wanted him to place his hands on the children and pray for them. But the disciples told them not to do it.**
> **Jesus said, 'Let the little children come to me. Don't keep them away. The kingdom of heaven belongs to people like them.' Jesus placed his hands on them to bless them…. "** Matthew 19:13-14.

WE BELIEVE CHILDREN CAN LEARN TO HEAR THE VOICE OF GOD AND MINISTER TO ONE ANOTHER. We once heard of a Bible school that allows children to minister in a special way. When one of the teachers is sick, they bring in the small children to have them lay hands on and pray for him. Then God heals the teacher! Children are helpers who God can use for good. You can hear God's voice, you can have visions, and you can powerfully share what you know about Jesus—the King of Kings.

We pray that you, your family and friends will be blessed by what you learn from this training course. We also pray that you will hear God's voice more and more clearly as you grow. Visit the ZOE website for more information: www.zoeministries.org.

John 10:27 (NKJV) says, **"My sheep hear My voice, and I know them, and they follow Me."** THIS SCRIPTURE DOESN'T APPLY JUST TO ADULTS, BUT TO *ALL* OF GOD'S PEOPLE. Take this scripture, apply it during this training course, and watch the Lord work!

In Christ,

Dick and Ginny Chanda

We are God's special creation.

Remember, you are to break this up into "bite size" pieces, depending upon the ages of your children. At this point, direct the children to close their Workbooks and take out their Bibles. We use the NIrV Adventure Bible for Early Readers Version.

1. *Help the children find and read aloud* **Genesis 1:1** *and* **Genesis 1:27.**
   Genesis 1:1 "In the beginning, God created the heavens and the earth."

   Genesis 1:27 "So God created human beings in his own likeness. He created them to be like himself. He created them as male and female."

   Ask: Did you know that God formed you to be like Him?
   What does it mean to you to be like God?
   [We love the things He created like animals, flowers, beaches, mountains and sunsets.]

   Ask: In what ways are we **NOT** like God?
   [We make mistakes, do things that are wrong, and can't make a star or planet.]

   Ask: Have you ever thought of how important you must be to God that He would want to make you like Himself?
   Do you feel important?

   Say: Well, you are very important and very special to Him.

2. *Find and read aloud* **Genesis 1:31a.**
   "God saw everything that he had made. And it was very good."

   Say: God loves people so much that when He created us, He was very pleased with what He had made. We are God's creation and He thinks each of us is special.

   Ask: Do you think you are special?
   [If a child answers yes, then agree that he is right. If he answers no, then take a moment to affirm him of his great value in this world. Tell him that God wants to show him that he is special to Him.]

   LA #1, AP #1

3. *Find and read aloud* **Psalm 139:17.**
   "God, your thoughts about me are priceless. No one can possibly add them all up."

   Say: Did you know that God thinks about you?

   God has been thinking of each of us from the moment He formed the earth and all that was on it. God knew each one of us before we were even born.

   LA #2

4. *Find and read aloud* **Jeremiah 1:5.**
   "Before I formed you in your mother's body I chose you. Before you were born I set you apart to serve me. I appointed you to be a prophet to the nations."

   Say: In this verse, God is speaking to a man named Jeremiah, who became a prophet. God also **CHOSE US** before we were formed inside our mother. Before we were born God set us apart to serve Him in some special way.

5. *Find and read aloud* **Psalm 139:16-17.**
   "Your eyes saw my body even before it was formed. You planned how many days I would live. You wrote down the number of them in your book, before I had lived through even one of them."

   Say: A man named David wrote this verse. He spent many hours with God and came to know Him well. This verse shows us that God knew what we would look like before He even created us. God has planned how many days we will live. When God created the earth, the animals, the plants and all the people, He thought of each one of us and He gave each of us a special purpose, or job.

   LA #3

6. *Find and read aloud* **Jeremiah 29:11.**
   "'I know the plans I have for you,' announces the Lord. 'I want you to enjoy success. I do not plan to harm you. I will give you hope for the years to come.'"

   Say: Sometimes people discover what plans God has for them when they are young, and some people wait until they are older to learn what God's plans are for them. However, God always wants each of us to get to know Him and become His close friend.

   LA #4

7. *Find and read aloud* **Jeremiah 29:12-13.**
   "Then you will call out to me. You will come and pray to me. And I will listen to you. When you look for me with all your heart, you will find me."

   Ask: So, how do we call out to God?
   [It is by praying—speaking to Him in our hearts or out loud.]

   LA #5

We are blessed by God to be a blessing.

1. *Find and read aloud* **Mark 10:14b-16.**
   "'Let the little children come to me. Don't keep them away. God's kingdom belongs to people like them. What I'm about to tell you is true. Anyone who will not receive God's kingdom like a little child will never enter it.' Then He took the children in His arms. He placed His hands on them to bless them."

   Or for younger children:
   "'Let the little children come to me...' Then He took the children in His arms. He placed His hands on them to bless them" Mark 10:14, 16.

   Ask: What does it mean to bless someone?
   [It means to ask God to do good things in that person's life.]

   Say: This scripture is about Jesus wanting children to come to Him so that He can bless them. During Bible times, it was common for priests and parents to speak a blessing over a child. They would ask God what He wanted to do in that child's life and then speak it out loud over the child like a prayer.

   LA #6, AP #2, AP #3

2. *Find and read aloud* **Numbers 6:24-26.**
"May the Lord bless you and take good care of you. May the Lord smile on you and be gracious to you. May the Lord look on you with favor and give you peace."

Say: This is the blessing that God gave to a priest in the Old Testament to speak over all of God's people.

LA #7

3. *Find and read aloud* **Genesis 12:2.**
"I will make you into a great nation. And I will bless you. I will make your name great. You will be a blessing to others."

Say: God spoke these words to Abraham. God's promise didn't seem possible to Abraham because his wife, Sarah, was not able to get pregnant. Abraham probably wondered, "How could my family grow big enough to finally become a whole nation of people if my wife can't have even one baby?"

Yet, God made it possible for Sarah to have a baby, even though she was very old. Their son, Isaac, had children, and then they had children, until Abraham's family became the nation of Israel. And God did bless Abraham with many sheep and cattle, as well as servants to help him take care of them. He became very rich.

Ask: What did God mean when He said, **"You will be a blessing to others"**?
[To be a blessing means to help or do something good for someone.]

Say: Abraham was a blessing to others. He helped many people. Much later, one of his descendants turned out to be Jesus, who we know is a blessing to others.

4. *Find and read aloud* **Galatians 3:7-9.**
"…Those who have faith are children of Abraham…God said, 'All nations will be blessed because of you.' So those who depend on faith are blessed along with Abraham."

Say: This verse says that WE can also be children of Abraham! It means that if we place our faith in Jesus, we also will be blessed by God and can be a blessing to others.

Ask: How can we bless another person?
[We can bless other people by saying something that encourages them, or helping them in some way. We can show them that we love them and God loves them.]

Say: God can use us to bless another person by telling us what to say to him that would help him. One important way to do this is to tell him about Jesus, so that Jesus can come into his life, forgive his sins and be his friend.

LA #8, LA #9

PRAYER AND MINISTRY TIME

Below are several short blessings for your use. Select one that seems most appropriate for each child, or ask God to give you a unique blessing for each child. Include in your blessing some of the positive ways God sees the child. Lay your hand on his shoulder, and speak a blessing over him. Jesus gave us the authority to use His mighty name, so you might seal each blessing by ending it with: "In Jesus' name, I pray."

Say: Today I am going to pray a blessing over you. I will ask the Lord to show me the best way to bless you.
Sample Blessings:

Lord, we thank you for _____. May he come to know You, Jesus, in a very special and wonderful way.

Jesus, we ask that you bless _____ with ears to hear Your voice and to have the courage to share with others what he knows about You.

We ask also that _____ will understand that You love him and that You take great delight in him.

Jesus, we bless _____ and ask that You help him know that he is created in Your image and that You take great pleasure in the way You made him!

Jesus, thank You that _____ is precious to You, and You are pleased to bless him as one of Your very special children.

Father, the Bible says that there is no fear in love and that Your perfect love makes fear disappear. Father, I ask that You pour Your perfect love on _____, and that he would know that he is loved by You.

Lord, I ask that _____ would give himself to You, to be holy, pure, and willing to be different from this world. May he be transformed as You allow him to think like You think.

Father, I ask that _____ would go through all the days of his life, amazed by You, knowing that You love him and are with him.

Jesus, the Bible says that respecting and wanting to please You is the beginning of being smart and wise, so I ask that _____ would respect You and hate sin the way You hate it.

Lord, bless _____ with good friends and relationships that show Your goodness.

Father, bless _____. Please protect him wherever he goes. May he have everything he really needs.

Father, Your Word says that Jesus became smarter and stronger as He grew, and that You and all people respected Him. So, I bless _____ and ask that he would became smarter and stronger as he grows and that he would be respected by You and other people.

Lord, help _____ keep You in his thoughts all day, because You will pour Your perfect peace on people who remember again and again who You are.

LEARNING ACTIVITIES
Activity #1 God says I am good.
In the Workbook, have the children write their name on the blank line in the verse **Genesis 1:31a**. Have them read the verse aloud with their name in it.

Activity #2 I am priceless to God.
MATERIALS NEEDED: A phone or computer connected to the internet

Search YouTube for a lyric video of "Priceless" by For King and Country. Have the children copy into the Workbook the lyrics in the song that seem important to them. Ask them what they think God is saying to them through this song. Have them write their thoughts in the Workbook.

Activity #3 Before I arrived
Tell the children that God knew what they would be like before they were born, and He is not surprised by who

they are. Have them make a list of the people who were waiting for them to arrive. Help them interview several people from their list, asking the following questions:

Did you know anything about me before I arrived? If so, what?
Are you surprised by what I look like, the personality I have, or what I like to do?

They should record the answers they were given in the Workbook.

Activity #4 Make a fruit salad together.
MATERIALS NEEDED: A large bowl, colander, knives, several different kinds of fruit.

Help the children wash, cut up and combine several different fruits in a bowl.

Say: God made each fruit in a special way. He had a plan for each kind of fruit. He made them all for us to enjoy, but they each have a special job or purpose. Each carries a vitamin, mineral or other nutrient to help us be healthy. In a way, we are like the fruit. We each have a special job that God has given us. Together, we are like God's fruit salad. We all are different, and He enjoys each one of us.

Activity #5 Your message to God
God invites us to call out to Him and He will listen to us (**Jeremiah 29:12-13**). Have the children write out something they want to say to God.

Activity #6 Jesus' blessing over you
Ask: If Jesus were right here with us, what would you like Him to say in a blessing over you? Have the children write it out in the Workbook.

Activity #7 God's blessing on His people
Say: We know by reading the following verse what God wants for every child of His.
"May the Lord bless you and take good care of you. May the Lord smile on you and be gracious to you. May the Lord look on you with favor and give you peace" Numbers 6:24-26.

Have the children write or draw what they think these verses mean.

Activity #8 Father Abraham
MATERIALS NEEDED: A phone or computer connected to the internet

Say: **Galatians 3:7-9** reads, **"…Those who have faith are children of Abraham…God said, 'All nations will be blessed because of you.' So those who depend on faith are blessed along with Abraham."** So, if you have placed your faith in Jesus, you are a child of Abraham.

Search YouTube for the song "Father Abraham." Type in the phrase "Father Abraham song with lyrics and actions." We suggest the animated video titled "Father Abraham Had Many Sons – Kids Praise & Worship Bible Song." Sing along and follow the actions on the video.

Activity #9 Be a blessing.
Have the children think of some ways that they could be a blessing to other people this week. Have them make a list of people they know and write what they could say or do to help each of them.

Have the children pick one of these people and do or say something that would help him. Have them write in their Workbooks, describing what they did and what happened.

ART PROJECTS

Project #1 Make a creation ribbon.
MATERIALS NEEDED: Construction paper, scissors, markers or crayons, safety pins, hot glue gun

Have the children trace the Lesson 1 ribbon pattern in the Workbook on colored construction paper. Have them make a Creation Ribbon, writing on it one of these phrases:

God's Special Creation or Designed By God or I Am Chosen. Glue a safety pin on the back, so that they can wear their creation ribbon.

Project #2 Jesus enjoys children.
MATERIALS NEEDED: Markers, crayons or colored pencils

Have the children color in the coloring page in the back of the Workbook that shows Jesus having fun with the children.

Project #3 Jesus blesses children.
MATERIALS NEEDED: Markers, crayons or colored pencils

Have the children draw a picture of Jesus blessing a child in the Workbook.

LESSON 2

JESUS IS OUR SHEPHERD

OBJECTIVE

God is our Good Shepherd, and Jesus gave up His life for us, His lambs. Like a shepherd, He knows each one of us and wants to help us. One way He does this is by speaking with us in our spirits so that we can hear and follow Him.

JESUS IS OUR SHEPHERD

LESSON 2 CONTENT OBJECTIVE

To understand that God is our Good Shepherd, and Jesus gave up His life for us, His lambs. Like a shepherd, He knows each one of us and wants to help us. One way He does this is by speaking with us in our spirits so that we can hear and follow Him.

LESSON 2 KEY SCRIPTURE

Each day read aloud this lesson's scripture. Have the children write it out in the Workbook in the space provided. Encourage them to memorize this lesson's verse by the end of the week. Challenge the children to recite it without reading it.

John 10:14-15 "I am the good shepherd. I know my sheep, and my sheep know me…And I give my life for the sheep."

LESSON 2 READING ASSIGNMENT

Chapters 3 and 4 in *Is That Really You, God?*
Some children will need you to read portions of the assigned reading to them, others can read the chapters on their own or take turns reading aloud as a group.

TEACHING CONTENT, LEARNING ACTIVITIES AND ART PROJECTS

These are the largest components of the lesson. Depending upon your children's ages, you will need to decide how much of each section to cover in any given day. Select Learning Activities and Art Projects that fit your children's abilities and interests. Feel free to be creative and have fun as you lead your children into a real relationship with the Lord Jesus.

PRAYER AND MINISTRY TIME

Remember to choose a person who will receive prayer and ministry for this lesson. Help the children record this person's name in their Workbook. You should each agree to ask God to tell you something that will encourage that person. Refer to the prayer and ministry section of the Introduction, as needed.

Jesus is Our Shepherd

TEACHING CONTENT

1. *Help the children find and read aloud* **John 10:11-13.**

    I am the good shepherd. The good shepherd gives his life for the sheep. The hired man is not the shepherd and does not own the sheep. So when the hired man sees the wolf coming, he leaves the sheep and runs away. Then the wolf attacks the flock and scatters it. The man runs away because he is a hired man. He does not care about the sheep.

    Ask: "What is a good shepherd like?"
    [He is brave. He is willing to risk getting killed by a wolf in order to save his sheep. He is strong and can defend his sheep from wild animals. He thinks each of his sheep is valuable. He cares about each one.]

    LA #1, LA #2, LA #3, AP #1, AP #2

2. *Find and read aloud* **John 10:2-4.**

    "The one who enters through the gate is the shepherd of the sheep…The sheep listen to his voice. He calls his own sheep by name and he calls them out. When he has brought out all his own sheep, he goes on ahead of them."

    Ask: What do we know about sheep?
    Do they need help?
    [Yes, without a shepherd the sheep might get lost, attacked by a wild animal or fall off a cliff.]

    Ask: What are some ways that a shepherd helps his sheep?
    What does he do for them?
    [• He protects them from wild animals. If a wolf comes, the shepherd is brave and fights it. He builds a sheepfold with branches to keep the sheep safe at night. He sleeps at the door of the sheepfold, so nothing can get in to hurt them. The sheepfold also keeps the sheep from leaving and getting lost.]
    [• In the morning, the shepherd finds them fields of good grass to eat. When they have nibbled the grass short, he moves the flock to better grass. He knows what kinds of plants are good for them to eat. He leads them to clear water.]
    [• He knows which sheep are strong and which sheep need more help. He knows which ones get into the most trouble.]
    [• The shepherd takes care of them when they are sick. If one of them breaks a leg, he carries it on his shoulders until it can walk again.]
    [• The shepherd wants to help His sheep. When the sheep follow his directions, they are kept safe.]

    Say: Jesus wants us to learn what His voice sounds like, so that He can keep us safe.

    LA #4

3. *Find and read aloud* **John 10:14-16.**

    I am the good shepherd. I know my sheep, and my sheep know me. They know me just as the Father knows me and I know the Father. And I give my life for the sheep. I have other sheep that do not belong to this sheep pen. I must bring them in too. They also will listen to my voice. There will be one flock and one shepherd.

Say: The good shepherd watches the lambs being born, and he names each one of them. The lambs learn what their shepherd's voice sounds like. They know him. God watched each of US being born. He wants us to learn what His voice sounds like so that we can listen to Him. Jesus wants everyone to be in His flock so that He can keep them safe and they can get to know Him. We become a sheep in Jesus' flock by believing that He is God's Son, who came to pay the penalty for our sins. Sins are those wrong things we have done.

4. *Find and read aloud* **John 3:16.**
"God so loved the world that he gave his one and only Son. Anyone who believes in him will not die but will have eternal life."

Say: When God sent His Son Jesus into this world, He did it because He loves us—He wants to come into our life and help us.

If all of the children have already accepted Jesus as their Savior, proceed to number 5. If you are not sure, ask the children if they have ever invited Jesus to come into their heart. If some have not, ask if they would like to. If so, explain that Jesus will come into their hearts as they honestly say they are sorry for the wrong things they have done, and then invite Jesus in. The children can invite Jesus in by saying an honest prayer to Him. Ask the children to repeat the following prayer after you if it says what they want to say to God.

Say: Dear God, I want Jesus in my heart. I'm sorry that I have done wrong things that You don't like. Thank You for forgiving me for all the things I've done wrong. Thank You for coming into my life and being my Shepherd. Thank you for knowing me and loving me. Amen.

If the children can read and understand scriptures, you may want to read through the "Salvation Scriptures" section in the back of their Workbook or this Parent/Teacher Training Guide. Go through those scriptures with interested children, and then ask if they want to ask Jesus into their heart. If they do, lead them in the prayer above. Those verses can also assure them of their salvation.

LA #5, LA #6

5. *Say:* When we invite Jesus to come into our hearts, His Holy Spirit comes to live inside us. Jesus called this being born again (**John 3:3**). God gives LIFE to our spirit!

Find and read aloud **Ezekiel 36:26-27.**
"I will give you a new heart and put a new spirit in you; I will remove from you your heart of stone and give you a heart of flesh. And I will put my Spirit in you and move you to follow my decrees and be careful to keep my laws."

Say: We can hear God's voice better when we become one of Jesus' sheep because it is IN OUR SPIRIT that we hear His Spirit speaking to us. Jesus, our Good Shepherd, knows each of us. He wants what is best for us, and He wants to help us. He can help us the most when we hear His voice and follow His directions. For us to hear God clearly, we need two things. First, we need to become one of His sheep by believing in Him, and second, we need to be READY TO LISTEN for His voice.

6. *Find and read aloud* **John 10:27.**
"My sheep listen to my voice, I know them, and they follow me" NIV.

Say: Let's look at three words that Jesus uses in this verse—listen, know and follow.

Ask: What does the word LISTEN mean?

[To listen means to hear and want to obey what you hear.[1] Jesus' sheep hear His voice AND they want to obey what He says.]

Say: The next word we will look at is KNOW. Jesus said that He knows us. **John 10:3** says, **"He calls his own sheep by name and he leads them out."** So, Jesus, our good Shepherd, knows our names.

Ask: How well do you think He knows you?
[Last week we talked about Jesus knowing us before we were even born! He knows how long we will live. He knows what we like; He knows what we don't like. He knows the dreams and hopes we have. He sees us when we are hurt, and He feels badly. He is proud of us when we do something that is difficult for us. He is proud when we do our best. That is how well Jesus knows us!]

Say: The last word we will look at is FOLLOW.

Ask: What did Jesus mean when He said that His sheep follow Him?
      What does the word follow mean?
[To follow means to do the same thing as someone else. It means to go the same way with someone. So, when we follow Jesus, we go through our day with Him and do the same thing He does.]

LA #7

7. *Find and read aloud* **John 10:4-5.**
"When he has brought out all his own sheep, he goes on ahead of them. His sheep follow him because they know his voice. But they will never follow a stranger. In fact, they will run away from him. They don't recognize a stranger's voice."

Say: Jesus is saying that sheep don't follow anyone but their own shepherd.

Read aloud the following story:
      An American, traveling in Syria, saw three native shepherds bring their flocks to the same brook, and the flock drank there together. At length one shepherd arose and called out, "Men-ah!" the Arabic for "Follow me." His sheep came out of the common herd and followed him up the hillside. The next shepherd did the same, and his sheep went away with him and the man did not even stop to count them.
      The traveler said to the remaining shepherd, "Give me your turban and crook, and see if they will not follow me as well as you." So he put on the shepherd's things and called out, "Men-ah! Men-ah!" Not a sheep moved.
      "They know not the voice of a stranger."
      "Will your flock never follow anybody but you?" inquired the gentleman. The Syrian shepherd replied, "Oh, yes; sometimes a sheep gets sick, and then he will follow anyone."[2]

Say: So all HEALTHY sheep will follow their shepherd.

LA #8

PRAYER AND MINISTRY TIME

Take turns sharing what the Lord has given you to share with the person receiving ministry. Allow time now to hear anything more that the Lord wants to say.

Review the Prayer and Ministry Time section of the Introduction, as needed.

LEARNING ACTIVITIES

Activity #1 Tell the story.
MATERIALS NEEDED: Construction paper and scissors, Lesson 2 story field patterns

Together, tell the story of the parable of the good shepherd and the hired hand. The story field can be made of a large circle of green paper. Using the Lesson 2 patterns provided in the Workbook, trace the patterns on construction paper and cut out the shapes to create the different characters and props. Trace and cut out branches from brown paper to build a sheepfold. Cut out large rock shapes from gray paper for the wolf to hide behind. Trace a wolf on black paper and cut it out. Trace several sheep on white paper and cut them out. Trace the shepherd and hired hand on different color paper so you can tell the difference between them.

First, you tell the parable in your own words, moving the pieces over the story field. The children can then tell the story. The children may want to present this parable to a friend or relative.

Activity #2 Act out the good shepherd and the hired hand parable.
MATERIALS NEEDED: Cardboard, construction paper and clothes, OR cardboard, scissors, string and markers

Together, act out the parable of the good shepherd and the hired hand, choosing parts of the good shepherd, the hired hand, sheep, and the wolf. Make props from construction paper and cardboard, and costumes from clothes you have. You could also just use one prop or piece of costume for each different character. Alternatively, you could make cardboard signs to tie around the neck, reading GOOD SHEPHERD, HIRED HAND, SHEEP and WOLF. Act out this story several times, changing parts.

Activity #3 David, the shepherd boy
MATERIALS NEEDED: A Bible

Read together **1 Samuel 17:32-37** to read about King David when he was a shepherd boy. Have the children write in their Workbook what they think about David. Was he a GOOD shepherd or not, and why?

Activity #4 Make a sheepfold.
MATERIALS NEEDED: Branches, cardboard boxes or other material to create a sheepfold

Have the children create a sheepfold out of sticks, cardboard or other materials. Have each child sit or lay down inside, imagining he is a sheep inside it.

Ask: In what ways does God protect you?
Have the children write in their Workbook some of the ways that God protects them.

Activity #5 Illustration for Jesus' cleansing blood

MATERIALS NEEDED: A glass jar, water, iodine and dropper, hydrogen peroxide, tablespoon measuring spoon, a spoon for stirring.

Say: This will show what happens whenever you ask Jesus to forgive your sin. *Start with a glass jar at least half-filled with water. Get ready a dropper of iodine.*

Say: I am that water. I just told a lie, so I'll add just a drop of iodine to the water. I stole a cookie from the cookie jar, so I'll add another drop of iodine to the water. I just pinched my sister, so I'll add another drop of iodine to the water. *Stir the water with a spoon, and watch the water turn brown.*

Say: They were just little sins, but they made ALL of me dirty. I need Jesus' blood to cleanse me from my sins. If I ask for His forgiveness, He will cleanse me of all my sin. *Get ready two tablespoons of hydrogen peroxide.*

Say: This is Jesus' blood. *Then pour it into the jar of brown water and stir.*

Say: Jesus' blood washes away ALL of my sin.

Activity #6 Watch a video about sheep and their shepherd.

MATERIALS NEEDED: A phone or computer with internet access

Search YouTube for a video titled "Do sheep only obey their Master's voice?" by Øyvind Kleiveland.

This is a video of a modern-day shepherd whose flock will only come when he calls.

Activity #7 Read a true story.

Read the following true story by Steve Lightle from his book, *Exodus II—Let My People Go.*

> I had read the verses in John 10 where four times Jesus said, "My sheep know My voice." **John 18:37** says, "*. . . Every one who is of the truth hears My voice.*" When I read these, I said, "Wow! I know You Jesus. I'm born of the truth. But, I need to hear Your voice, Lord!" And so I said, "Oh, Lord, I want to hear Your voice! I want to hear Your voice! Speak to me!"
>
> Even though He had spoken to me on several other occasions, it was something that seemed so rare. I wanted to have daily fellowship and communion with Jesus so that I could hear His voice regularly.
>
> Then one night—a cold night in February—Judy and I were sleeping as usual with the windows open. There was snow on the ground and it seemed almost colder inside the room than outside. At about 2:30 a.m., all of a sudden I was wide awake. This was very unusual for me. Normally, I can sleep through anything. I thought, "What in the world am I doing awake?" Then it dawned on me that maybe it was the Lord's doing.
>
> "Lord, did You wake me up?"
>
> And that still inner voice spoke to me and said, "Yes, son."
>
> That response was really something. I remember how there was such a settling of security in my heart when the Lord said "son." It established who He is and who I am. He's my Father and I'm His son.
>
> "Oh, Lord, what do You want?" I said.
>
> And the Lord spoke in a very clear voice in my heart and He said, "I want you to get out of bed. I want you to lie on the floor because I have something I want to tell you."
>
> "Lord," I said, "I'll just lie right here in my nice warm bed and You can tell me what You want to tell me. It would be cold if I got out and laid on the floor."
>
> "No," the Lord said. "I told you to get up, get out of bed, and lie down on the floor because I have something to tell you."

"Lord, no," I argued. "Tell me why. I want to stay here in this warm bed." This exchange went on several times.

The Lord got rather stern with me in His voice. Finally I said, "Okay, I'll do it." And so I got up out of bed and it was cold! The Lord had told me to lie at the foot of the bed, which was hardwood flooring. And I thought, "Oh, this is really going to be cold!" And when I went there and laid down, God had supernaturally heated the spot on the floor. It was as though I was lying on a beach in Hawaii. I was so thrilled!

If I hadn't been obedient and gotten up out of that bed, I would have missed that experience.

I began to worship and praise the Lord. I lost track of time. Then I remembered. "Lord, You wanted to tell me something. What is it You wanted to tell me?"

"I wanted to tell you that you could get up and go back to bed."

"What?" I was shocked.

"Yes, you can get up and get into bed."

"I don't understand," I complained. "You tell me to get out of bed. I get out. You said to lie down at the foot of the bed. I laid down here. And now You tell me the thing You wanted to tell me was that I could go back and get in bed?"

"Yes," He said. "I wanted to see if you would obey Me. It's not just good enough to hear My voice. I wanted to see if you would obey me in something small."

The Lord taught me that if I would be obedient to His voice in the little things, then He would begin to give me other more important opportunities. I didn't realize that there would be a time coming in my life when that same voice that tested me and taught me that night would be the one that would speak to me when I was ministering behind the Iron Curtain and say, "Don't go to that place," and it would save my life.[3]

Ask: What did you learn about God from this true story?

Why did God wake up that man to talk to him?

Have the children write their thoughts about this story in the Workbook.

Activity #8 Watch a video about Jesus washing away our sins.

MATERIALS NEEDED : A phone or computer connected to the internet

Search YouTube for the video titled "A science experiment showing how Christ can wash away our sins" by Robert Nollkamper.

ART PROJECTS

Project #1 The Hireling Fleeth (The Hired Hand Runs Away) coloring page

MATERIALS NEEDED: Crayons, markers or colored pencils

Have the children color in The Hireling Fleeth coloring page. Ask them, "What can you learn from this picture?"

Project #2 God took care of me.

MATERIALS NEEDED: Crayons, markers or colored pencils

Ask the children to think about times when God protected or took care of them. Have them draw a picture of one of those times.

LESSON 3

LISTEN, KNOW AND FOLLOW

OBJECTIVE

Because we are children of God, we can learn how to listen, recognize and follow God's leading. We can recognize when God is speaking to us by comparing what we hear with what God has already spoken in the Bible.

LISTEN, KNOW AND FOLLOW

LESSON 3 CONTENT OBJECTIVE

To understand that because the children are children of God, they can learn how to listen, recognize and follow God's leading. They can recognize when God is speaking to them by comparing what they hear with what God has already spoken in the Bible.

LESSON 3 KEY SCRIPTURE

Each day read aloud this lesson's scripture. Have the children write it out in the Workbook in the space provided. Encourage the children to memorize this lesson's verse by the end of the week. Challenge them to recite it without reading it.

John 10:27 "My sheep listen to my voice, I know them, and they follow me" NIV.

LESSON 3 READING ASSIGNMENT

Read Chapter 5 in *Is That Really You, God?*
Some children will need you to read portions of the assigned reading to them, others can read the chapters on their own or take turns reading aloud as a group.

TEACHING CONTENT, LEARNING ACTIVITIES AND ART PROJECTS

These are the largest components of the lesson. Depending upon your children's ages, you will need to decide how much of each section to cover in any given day. Select Learning Activities and Art Projects that fit your children's abilities and interests. Feel free to be creative and have fun as you lead your children into a real relationship with the Lord Jesus.

PRAYER AND MINISTRY TIME

Remember to choose a person who will receive prayer and ministry for this lesson. Help the children record this person's name in their Workbook. You should each agree to ask God to tell you something that will encourage that person. Refer to the prayer and ministry section of the Introduction, as needed.

Listen, Know and Follow

TEACHING CONTENT

Listen for God's voice.

1. *Ask:* What does it mean to **EXPECT** something?
   [It means to believe that something will happen. For example, when it is your birthday, you expect family to give you a present.]

   Say: If you have accepted Jesus into your life, you are a child of God. If you are a child of God, you can **EXPECT** God to lead you.

   Help the children find and read aloud **Romans 8:14** and **John 8:47**.
   Romans 8:14 "Those who are led by the Spirit of God are children of God."

   John 8:47 "He who belongs to God hears what God says."

2. *Say:* Let's talk about what we can do to hear God more often and more clearly.

   a. Talk to Jesus, praying either aloud or silently in your heart. Spend time listening. You can ask God a question and give Him time to answer you.

   b. Read what God has already said in the Bible. As you read, see if the Holy Spirit makes a verse or passage stand out for you.

   c. Write in a journal what you think He is saying to you. Sometimes He will speak as you write.

   d. Spend time singing worship songs, expressing your love for Him. He may speak to you during times of worship.

   e. Spend time with other Christians by going to church and studying the Bible together. God may speak to you through them.

   LA #1, LA #2

Recognize God's Voice.

1. *Say*: People tell us what to do everywhere we go. Television commercials and ads on the internet tell us what to buy. Friends tell us what they think we should do. The radio announces events we could go to. Announcements at church talk about chances to volunteer and help others. One goal of this course is to help us pick out, or recognize, God's voice among all the voices, so that we can follow Him. We want to follow God's voice because He wants the best for us. He has great things planned for us to do.
   The more often we hear someone's voice, the easier it is to know who it is. It is the same with God. The more often we spend time with Him, the easier it will be to recognize His voice. The better we get to know Him over time, the easier it will be to know when it is He who is speaking to us.

2. *Find and read aloud* **Romans 8:16.**
   "The Spirit himself testifies with our spirit that we are God's children."

Say: We can depend on the Holy Spirit to tell us in our spirit what God is saying. Knowing God's voice takes some practice. But God is patient, and He will give us many chances to hear and recognize His voice. When we hear an idea, we need to see if it is from God or not. The Holy Spirit inside us helps us know if it is God's idea.

One way to RECOGNIZE what God wants is to read what He says in the Bible. If we hear something that is the opposite of what God says in the Bible, then we know that it is NOT God speaking to us. The more time we spend reading our Bible, the more we will see the goodness of God. When we get an idea to do something good, it could be God giving us that thought. What He says sounds good just like He is good!

When we hear and recognize God speaking, we should do what He says. If someone tells us to do something that God would not want, we should not do it.

LA #3

3. *Say:* Let's talk about what God might say to us.

   a. *Find and read aloud* **Galatians 5:22.**
     "But the fruit the Holy Spirit produces is love, joy and peace. It is being patient, kind and good. It is being faithful and gentle and having control of oneself...."

     Say: God wants us to be led by His Holy Spirit. **Galatians 5:22** talks about what the Holy Spirit likes and what kind of person He will lead us to become. Often we can recognize God's Holy Spirit inside us, encouraging us to be loving, joyful, peacemakers, etc.

   b. *Find and read aloud* **John 14:31.**
     "...I love the Father. They must also learn that I do exactly what my Father has commanded me to do."

     Say: Jesus was obedient to God the Father because He loved His Father. God wants us to be like Jesus. We know how Jesus lived while on earth by reading the Bible books **Matthew, Mark, Luke** and **John**. So, if we have a thought or hear a suggestion to act like Jesus, we RECOGNIZE it is God speaking.

     Ask: How did Jesus ACT?
          What did He do?
     [• He loved people.]
     [• He patiently taught people.]
     [• He helped people in need.]
     [• He stood up for what was right.]
     [• He said No to evil.]
     [• He invited people to believe in Him.]

   c. *Say*: We know one thing that God always wants. It is to bring more sheep into His flock, where He can take care of them. He loves people and He wants what is best for them. So, if we have the thought that maybe we should become a friend to someone, so that they can hear about Jesus, it could be God speaking to us. We RECOGNIZE that it is something Jesus likes to do.

LA #4

Follow God's Voice.

1. *Find and read aloud* **John 10:27.**
   "My sheep listen to my voice, I know them, and they follow me."

   Say: Jesus said this to all His followers. We, as God's sheep, should hear and obey Jesus' voice. We want to follow Jesus. A good rule to remember is: *It is better to follow and fail than fail to follow!*

   Ask: What does this mean?
   [It is better to try to follow what we THINK God is saying, than to not try at all! God really likes it when we TRY to follow Him. If we don't even try, He is disappointed.]

2. *Find and read aloud* **John 8:31.**
   "If you obey my teaching, you are really my disciples."

   Say: While Jesus was on earth, He had disciples who came to know and love Him. They believed He was the Son of God, the Messiah, the One who came to save us. They followed Him, trying to live as He taught them. He was saying that His disciples are the people who OBEY His teachings.

   So, WE can be Jesus' disciples too, if we obey His teachings in the Bible. Obeying Jesus shows that we love Him.

   LA #5, LA #6, LA #7, LA #8

3. *Find and read aloud the following verses.*
   Hebrew 3:7-8 "The Holy Spirit says, 'Listen to his voice today. If you hear it, don't be stubborn….'"

   Hebrew 3:15 "It has just been said, 'Listen to his voice today. If you hear it, don't be stubborn. You were stubborn when you opposed me.'"

   Hebrews 4:7 "Listen to his voice today. If you hear it, don't be stubborn."

   Say: These verses talk about listening to God and BEING WILLING to follow Him.

   Ask: What does it mean to be stubborn?
   [A person who is stubborn insists on doing things HIS way. He will NOT CHANGE even if he is given a good reason to change. A good picture of being stubborn is a mule sitting down in the road, refusing to be led anywhere by his owner.]

4. *Find and read aloud* **Psalm 32:8-9.**
   "I will guide you and teach you the way you should go. I will give you good advice and watch over you with love. Don't be like a horse or a mule. They can't understand anything. They have to be controlled by bit and bridles. If they aren't, they won't come to you."

   Say: We can really hear God's heart in these verses. He wants us to understand that He gives good advice and watches over us with love. He wants to guide and teach us the way to go.

   If we are stubborn like a mule and refuse to listen and obey, we have a hard heart. It is difficult to hear God

---

when our heart is hard. We need to keep our hearts soft toward God, and be willing to listen. Because we are sheep in Jesus' flock, we will become better and better at listening to His voice and following Him. We can ask God for help to hear and obey Him. We know He wants to help us.

AP #1

PRAYER AND MINISTRY TIME:

Take turns sharing what the Lord has given you to share with the person receiving ministry. Allow time now to hear anything more that the Lord wants to say.

Review the Prayer and Ministry Time section of the Introduction, as needed.

LEARNING ACTIVITIES

Activity #1 Ways to hear God more often and more clearly

Below are ways that we can better hear God speaking to us:

a. Talk to Jesus, praying either aloud or silently in your heart. Spend time listening. You can ask God a question and give Him time to answer you.

b. Read what God has already said in the Bible. As you read, see if the Holy Spirit makes a verse or passage stand out for you.

c. Write in a journal what you think He is saying to you. Sometimes He will speak as you write.

d. Spend time singing worship songs, expressing your love for Him. He may speak to you during times of worship.

e. Spend time with other Christians by going to church and studying the Bible together. God may speak to you through them.

Ask: Have you heard from God through some of these ways? Which ones?
    What new way would you like to try out?

Have the children write out their answers in their Workbook.

Activity #2 Play "God Says."

Play a game of Simon Says but call it "God Says," so that the children can practice listening and obeying.

You play the part of the leader, or "God." The children are the players. Standing in front of the group, tell players what they must do. They must only obey commands that begin with the words "God Says." If you say, "God says, touch your nose," then players must touch their nose. But, if you simply say, "Jump," WITHOUT first saying "God says," players must not jump. Those that do jump are "out" and must sit down.

The players' goal is to follow directions and stay in the game for as long as possible! The last player standing wins and becomes the next leader, or "God." The leader's goal is to help the players to practice listening and obeying. This game can be repeated several times.

Activity #3 Play "Guess Who."
MATERIALS NEEDED : A blindfold and a telephone that can send and receive text messages

In this game the player tries to recognize who is speaking to him. Place a blindfold over the player's eyes, so that he cannot see who is speaking. If there is a person in the room who the player does not know well, have that person say, "Can you guess who I am?" Then have someone the player knows well say, "Can you guess who I am?"

Ask: "Whose voice was easier to recognize? Was it easier to recognize the person you have spent more time with?" Take turns being the blindfolded player.

A variation is to use your phone to text several people who are not present in turn, some more or less familiar to the player, asking them to call and ask, "Can you guess who I am?"

Activity #4 God is our good Father.
MATERIALS NEEDED: A computer or telephone that has internet access

Search YouTube for the song "Good, Good Father" by Chris Tomlin. Have the children listen to the song and read the lyrics.

Ask: Which parts of this song talk about hearing from God? What part of the song seems important for you to remember?

Have the children write out their answers in their Workbook.

Activity #5 Obedience that pleases God or blind obedience?
Discuss the game Simon Says (God Says).

Ask: What is the difference between the type of obedience Christians are supposed to have (obey what God says is true and right) and "blind obedience" (doing whatever you are told)?

Have the children write out examples of both types of obedience in their Workbook.

Activity #6 Play "Mother, May I?"
Play the game "Mother, May I?" in order to practice following directions.

One player is designated as the Mother—it can be a girl or a boy—and all the others are considered children. Standing on opposite sides of a room or field, the children take turns asking, "Mother, may I _____?" filling the blank with a requested movement. For example, one might ask, "Mother, may I take five steps forward?" Mother replies, "Yes, you may" or "No, you may not, but instead you may take _____," and adds a command. The child MUST follow the command from the Mother, whether it leads the child closer to or farther from the goal of reaching Mother. The children who forget to ask, "Mother, may I?" must return to the starting line. The first child to reach the Mother wins the game and becomes the Mother.

The children may ask Mother for permission to make some of the following movements.
"Mother, may I _____?"
• Take (a number) steps forward
• Take (a number) giant steps forward
• Take (a number) baby steps forward
• Run forward for (a number) seconds
• Crabwalk forward for (a number) seconds

If Mother does not approve the requests, she might give a command to:
• Reduce the child's request, e.g., Mother could reduce five giant steps to three giant steps.
• Take (a number) steps backward
• Run backward for (a number) seconds

Activity #7 Is God like the "Mother" in Mother, May I?
Discuss what happens during the game "Mother, May I?"

Ask: How is this "Mother" like God, and how is this "Mother" NOT like God?
[Sometimes God seems like the "Mother" in this game when He has us go back and redo something or wait to move forward in our life. God is NOT like "Mother" because He does not force us to obey or else we get kicked out of the game. Plus, a certain person playing the "Mother" could make a player go backwards just to be mean. God is not mean. He loves us and always wants what is best for each of us.]

Activity #8 Take the good shepherd obstacle course.
MATERIALS NEEDED: A blindfold and large objects for an obstacle course

Make an obstacle course with large objects like chairs or tables. The idea of this game is to get through the course without running into an obstacle. Take turns being blindfolded. The teacher will be the voice of the good shepherd. The blindfolded child is moved away from the obstacle course and spun around a couple of times. The good shepherd will carefully guide each child through the course using only spoken commands. That child must listen closely to the shepherd's voice so that he can follow directions and not hit any obstacles. If the child is very skilled, others could make some noise as a distraction, to make it harder.

Say: We play this game to remind us that Jesus will guide us with His voice through the obstacles in life. He will meet each one of us where we are, so that as long as we are listening to Him, we will make it. Some of us may need to have the shepherd take us by the hand to help us through, which is what Jesus will do with us when we need it. When we become very good at following Jesus' directions, we will be able to pick out His voice among many voices.

ART PROJECT

Project #1 "Stubborn as a Mule"
MATERIALS NEEDED: Markers, crayons or colored pencils

Re-read **Psalm 32:8-9: "I will guide you and teach you the way you should go. I will give you good advice and watch over you with love. Don't be like a horse or a mule. They can't understand anything. They have to be controlled by bit and bridles. If they aren't, they won't come to you."** Briefly repeat the idea of being stubborn and not willing to listen to or obey God. Have your child draw an illustration for this passage.

LESSON 4

NOAH HEARD AND OBEYED

OBJECTIVE

Noah was a righteous man who heard God speaking to him. He did not stop obeying God because of what others said, and Noah didn't depend only on his own limited thinking. Noah knew God, and he trusted God to help him do what seemed impossible—to build an ark. Because he obeyed God's voice, God was able to save him, his family and the animals.

NOAH HEARD AND OBEYED

LESSON 4 CONTENT OBJECTIVE

To understand that Noah was a righteous man who heard God speaking to him. He did not stop obeying God because of what others said, and Noah didn't depend only on his own limited thinking. Noah knew God, and he trusted God to help him do what seemed impossible—to build an ark. Because he obeyed God's voice, God was able to save him, his family and the animals.

LESSON 4 KEY SCRIPTURE

Each day read aloud this lesson's scripture. Have the children write it out in the Workbook in the space provided. Encourage the children to memorize this lesson's verse by the end of the week. Challenge them to recite it without reading it.

Genesis 6:13-22 "Noah did everything just as God commanded him" 6:22.

LESSON 4 READING ASSIGNMENT

Read Chapters 6 and 7 in *Is That Really You, God?*

Some children will need you to read portions of the assigned reading to them, others can read the chapters on their own or take turns reading aloud as a group.

TEACHING CONTENT, LEARNING ACTIVITIES AND ART PROJECTS

These are the largest components of the lesson. Depending upon your children's ages, you will need to decide how much of each section to cover in any given day. Select Learning Activities and Art Projects that fit your children's abilities and interests. Feel free to be creative and have fun as you lead your children into a real relationship with the Lord Jesus.

PRAYER AND MINISTRY TIME

Remember to choose a person who will receive prayer and ministry for this lesson. Help the children record this person's name in their Workbook. You should each agree to ask God to tell you something that will encourage that person. Refer to the prayer and ministry section of the Introduction, as needed.

Noah Heard and Obeyed

TEACHING CONTENT

Noah listened to God.

1. *Say*: Today's lesson is about Noah. Let's read about what the world was like when Noah lived.

   Help the children find and read aloud **Genesis 6:5-7**.
   The Lord saw how bad the sins of everyone on earth had become. They only thought about evil things. The Lord was very sad that he had made human beings on the earth. His heart was filled with pain. So the Lord said, "I created human beings, but I will wipe them out. I will also destroy the animals, the birds in the sky, and the creatures that move along the ground. I am very sad that I made human beings."

   Ask: So, what was it like when Noah lived?
   [The people thought only about evil things.]
   Did you know God could be sad like we are sad?
   Do you think that God can also be happy like we are happy?
   Why was God so sad?
   [God was sad because most of the people chose to disobey Him and did evil things.]

2. *Find and read aloud* **Genesis 6:8-10**.
   "But the Lord was very pleased with Noah. Here is the story of Noah's family line. Noah was a godly man. He was without blame among the people of his time. He walked faithfully with God. Noah had three sons. Their names were Shem, Ham and Japheth."

   Ask: Why was God pleased with Noah?
   [Noah was a godly man.]
   What does it mean to be a godly person?
   [To be a godly person means that you talk, think and act in ways that please God.]

3. *Say*: The Bible shows that God prepares the hearts of His people before He gives them directions to do something new. God spoke to Noah's ancestors of something bad that would happen, and God prepared Noah's heart before telling him to build the ark. God began to reveal His plans through the names of the men in Noah's family, who were born before Noah.

   a. His great-great-grandfather's name was Jared, which means to go down or throw down.[1] This was the first warning of bad news to come.

   b. *Find and read aloud* **Genesis 5:22**.
      "Enoch walked faithfully with God 300 years after Methusaleh was born."

   Say: Enoch was Noah's great-grandfather. His name means to walk up and down and talk with someone.[2] Today we read that Noah also walked faithfully with God.

   Ask: What does it mean to walk faithfully with God?
   [To walk with God means that you go through life with God. You make a habit of talking together all day long. You enjoy the same things, and you are sad about the same things. When you walk with God, you try to live every day in a way that pleases Him.]

   c. Noah's grandfather's name was Methusaleh, which means "when he is dead, it shall come."[3] God was warning them that when Methusaleh died, something bad would happen. The Lord let Methusaleh live

969 years! God was very patient. He was hoping the people would change their evil ways during Methuselah's lifetime, but they didn't.

d. Noah's father's name was **Lamech**, which means "destroyer."[4] Lamech died five years before the flood that would destroy most of the people and animals on earth.

e. Find and read aloud **Genesis 5:29**.
"[Lamech] named him Noah. Lamech said, 'He will comfort us when we are working. He'll comfort us when our hands work so hard they hurt. We have to work hard because the Lord put a curse on the ground.'"

Say: Lamech and his wife had a baby, who they named Noah, which means "rest or comfort."[5] In this verse, Noah's father talked about what had happened in the Garden of Eden.

f. *Find and read aloud* **Genesis 3:17**.
The Lord God said to Adam, "You listened to your wife's suggestion. You ate fruit from the tree I warned you about. I said, 'You must not eat its fruit.' So I am putting a curse on the ground because of what you did. All the days of your life you will have to work hard. It will be painful for you to get food from the ground.'"

Say: Adam and Eve sinned by disobeying God. God really hates sin. He knows that sin hurts the people He has created. However, God had a plan to do something about sin. He would start over with human beings through Noah's family because Noah walked faithfully with God. Later, God would send His Son Jesus to pay the price for our sins by dying in our place. Because Noah heard God and obeyed, Jesus was eventually born.

4. *Find and read aloud* **Amos 3:7**.
"Surely the Sovereign Lord does nothing without revealing his plan to his servants the prophets."

Say: Before God does something big, He always speaks to His prophets so that they can tell His people. Noah was the person God spoke to about the coming flood. He told Noah exactly what to do.

5. *Find and read aloud* **Genesis 6:11-21**.

Say: It does not say **HOW** God spoke to Noah, but many people think that it was by a clear voice that seemed loud enough for others to hear it (the authoritative voice).

We **DO** know that God spoke with words, and He gave very specific directions. We also know that Noah heard these words in his spirit, or inner man—not in his mind. We know this because what Noah heard didn't make sense to him. He would not have thought up this idea himself. No one had ever heard of such a big flood that it would cover the whole earth! When God speaks to you, it won't **ALWAYS** make sense at first. Sometimes it makes sense right away, and sometimes it doesn't.

Noah obeyed God.

1. *Find and read aloud* **Genesis 6:13-22**.
"Noah did everything just as God commanded him" Genesis 6:22.

Ask: What questions or doubts do you think would come into your mind if God told you to build an ark to escape a big flood?
Say: Once Noah heard God in his spirit, he didn't **ALLOW** any questions or doubts in his mind to keep him from obeying God.

LA #1, LA #2, LA #3

2. *Find and read aloud* **2 Peter 2:5.**
   "…But Noah preached about the right way to live. God kept him safe. He also saved seven others."

   Say: Noah must have tried to warn his neighbors about the flood that would come. Unfortunately, only his family listened and was saved. Noah didn't let his neighbors, who didn't believe, talk him out of obeying God. Instead, he told his neighbors about the right way to live. While Noah and his family built the ark, their neighbors probably didn't understand what they were doing.

   Ask: How do you think Noah and his family felt when everyone else thought they were crazy?
   When you are in a situation where others think you are crazy because of what you believe, what do you say?

3. *Find and read aloud* **Hebrews 11:7.**
   "By faith Noah, when warned about things not yet seen, in holy fear built an ark to save his family. By his faith he condemned the world and became heir of the righteousness that comes by faith."

   Say: So when God spoke to Noah, his faith in God became strong. When God speaks to US, it will strengthen OUR faith.

4. *Find and read aloud* **John 15:15.**
   "I no longer call you servants, because a servant does not know his master's business. Instead, I have called you friends, for everything that I learned from my Father I have made known to you."

   Say: Jesus told his disciples everything the Father taught Him. Today, the Lord reveals things to us because we love Jesus and have His Holy Spirit living inside us.

   Ask: Has God ever revealed something to you before it happened, in order to prepare you?

5. *Find and read aloud* **Genesis 7:1-5.**
   Then the Lord said to Noah, "Go into the ark with your whole family. I know that you are a godly man among the people of today. Take seven pairs of every kind of 'clean' animal with you. Take a male and a female of each kind. Take one pair of every kind of animal that is not 'clean.' Take a male and female of each kind. Also take seven pairs of every kind of bird. Take a male and a female of each kind. Then every kind will be kept alive. They can spread out again over the whole earth. Seven days from now I will send rain on the earth. It will rain for 40 days and 40 nights. I will destroy from the face of the earth every living creature I have made."
   Noah did everything the Lord commanded him to do.

   Say: God told Noah to take his family into the ark and to bring with him "clean" and "unclean" animals (**Genesis 7:2**). God told him to bring seven pairs of "clean" animals so that some could be used for sacrifices (**8:20**) and one pair of "unclean" animals (**6:19; 7:2**).

   Once Noah heard God in his spirit, he didn't allow any questions or doubts in his mind to keep him from obeying God. Noah believed God would help him get the animals on the ark (**Genesis 6:22; 7:5**).

   Ask: What questions or doubts do you think would come into your mind if God told you to put all those wild animals on the ark?

   LA #4, AP #1

6. *Find and read aloud* **Genesis 7:6-10.**

> Noah was 600 years old when the flood came on the earth. He and his sons entered the ark. His wife and his sons' wives went with them. They went into the ark to escape the waters of the flood. Male and female pairs of "clean" animals and pairs of animals that were not "clean" came to Noah. So did male and female pairs of birds and all of the creatures that move along the ground. All of them came to Noah and entered the ark. Everything happened just as God had commanded Noah. After seven days the flood came on the earth.

Say: Noah only had one week to load all the animals on the ark (**Genesis 7:4, 10**).

Ask: How do you think God got the animals to come to Noah?

7. *Find and read aloud* **Genesis 7:13-16.**

> On that same day Noah entered the ark together with his sons Shem, Ham and Japheth. Noah's wife and the wives of his three sons also entered it. They had every kind of wild animal with them. They had every kind of livestock, creature that moves along the ground, and bird that flies. Pairs of all living creatures that breathe came to Noah and entered the ark. The animals going in were male and female of every living thing. Everything happened just as God had commanded Noah. Then the Lord shut him in.

Say: As Noah believed, God enabled the animals to come to him (**Genesis 6:20; 7:8–9, 15**). God even shut the door in the side of the ark for Noah. God must have opened the door after the flood, too. God gave Noah supernatural help. God asked Noah to do the impossible—and then He helped Noah to do it. This is how God works. When He tells us to do something, He helps us do it.

Ask: Has God told you to do something that seemed impossible?

LA #5, AP #2

God carried out His plan.

1. *Find and read aloud* **Genesis 7:4** and then **Genesis 7:10-12.**
Genesis 7:4 "Seven days from now I will send rain on the earth. It will rain for 40 days and 40 nights. I will destroy from the face of the earth every living creature I have made."

Genesis 7:10-12 "And after seven days the floodwaters came on the earth. Noah was 600 years old. It was the 17th day of the second month of the year. On that day all of the springs at the bottom of the ocean burst open. God opened the windows of the sky. Rain fell on the earth for 40 days and 40 nights."

Say: God did what He said He would do.

2. *Find and read aloud* **Genesis 7:23** and then **Genesis 8:1.**
Genesis 7:23 "Every living thing on earth was wiped out. People and animals were destroyed. The creatures that move along the ground and the birds in the sky were wiped out. Everything on earth was destroyed. Only Noah and those with him in the ark were left."

Genesis 8:1 "But God showed concern for Noah. He also showed concern for all the wild animals and livestock that were with Noah in the ark. So God sent a wind to sweep over the earth. And the waters began to go down."

Say: It is very sad that God had to destroy most of the people and animals on earth. God cared for Noah, his family and the surviving animals. The waters continued to go down, and the ark finally rested on the mountains of Ararat.

Noah waited for God's timing.

1. *Find and read aloud* **Genesis 8:6-17.**

   Say: Perhaps Noah didn't want to let the animals out of the ark until the earth was dry enough for them to be safe and find food. So, Noah sent out a raven first. Ravens will eat dead fish, frogs, mussels and clams, which would have been plentiful as the waters went down.[6] Ravens don't care if they sit on slimy ground. Noah's raven didn't come back to the ark because it found plenty of food to eat (**Genesis 8:7**).

   Then Noah sent out a dove. The dove serves as a symbol of holiness and purity. It doesn't like to land on wet, slimy ground. It will not eat dead animals. Doves eat seeds, fruit, grains and insects.[7] Noah's dove returned to the ark because it found no place to land and no food. **Genesis 8:9** says that Noah **"reached out his hand and took the dove in. He brought it back to himself in the ark."**

   Noah waited seven more days and sent the dove out a second time. This time the dove returned with an olive leaf in its beak. Noah took the dove back into the ark and waited another seven days. The third time Noah sent out the dove, the dove did not return (**Genesis 8:12**).

2. *Say:* Noah was careful to do things in God's timing. He built the ark when God told him to, even though it made no sense to his neighbors (**Genesis 6:22**). Also, Noah waited to send out the dove for another seven days (**Genesis 8:12**).

   Ask: How do you think you would have felt about waiting all this time?
   Would you have been eager to get off that stinky boat?

3. *Find and read aloud* **Genesis 8:15-18.**
   Then God said to Noah, "Come out of the ark. Bring your wife and your sons and their wives with you. Bring out every kind of living thing that is with you. Bring the birds, the animals, and all the creatures that move along the ground. Then they can multiply on the earth. They can have little ones and the number of them can increase."
   So Noah came out of the ark. His sons and his wife and his sons' wives were with him.

   Say: Noah did not get off the ark until God told him to and let him know it was safe. Noah and his family lived in the ark for more than a year!

   AP #3, AP #4

God was pleased with Noah's obedience.

1. *Say:* When Noah and his family got off the ark, Noah worshipped God and offered a burnt sacrifice to Him, to show how thankful he was to be saved from the flood.

   Find and read aloud **Genesis 8:21.**
   "The Lord smelled the pleasing aroma…."

   Say: This lesson began with God feeling terrible that He had made man, and it is ending with God being pleased with Noah's obedience and worship.

2. *Say:* Noah is a good example of an obedient man. He obeyed God, even though he didn't understand completely. The idea of a flood covering the whole earth would not have been an easy idea to understand at that time, but Noah obeyed and built the ark.

   Ask: When we respond to the Lord with obedience, how do you think it makes Him feel?
   When you have been obedient to God's Word, how do you feel?

3. *Say:* Because Noah recognized God's voice in his spirit and he was willing to follow that guidance, Noah pleased God and saved his family and many animals. God was so pleased with Noah that He made a promise to him. God promised He would never again send a worldwide flood to destroy the earth. A rainbow is a sign from God of this promise (**Genesis 9:8-17**). No matter how evil people become, God will never send a worldwide flood again.

   Ask: Aren't you glad God made that promise?

4. *Say:* Trusting God and following His directions of **WHAT** to do, **HOW** to do it, and **WHEN** to do it will help our families and us. God promises to bless the families of those who obey Him (**Psalm 112:1–2; Jeremiah 32:38–39**).

5. *Find and read aloud* **2 Chronicles 16:9a.**
   "The Lord looks out over the whole earth. He gives strength to those who commit their lives completely to him."

   Say: God looks for people like Noah, who give their hearts and lives to Him.

   Ask: What do you think it would look like to commit your whole life to God?

6. God loves speaking to us through His Holy Spirit inside us, but it is up to us to recognize God's voice and obey Him.

   LA #6, AP #5

PRAYER AND MINISTRY TIME

Take turns sharing what the Lord has given you to share with the person receiving ministry.
Allow time now to hear anything more that the Lord wants to say.

Review the Prayer and Ministry Time section of the Introduction, as needed.

LEARNING ACTIVITIES

Activity #1 Make a model of the ark.
MATERIALS NEEDED: Tag board, masking tape, yardstick and scissors

Help the children make a model of the ark following God's instructions in **Genesis 6:15-16 NIRV**. The scale is 450 feet = 4.5 feet long (54 inches), 75 feet wide = .75 feet (9 inches), and 45 feet high = .45 feet (5 ½ inches). Note: Various cubit lengths were used throughout history, which accounts for any differing measurements you might see elsewhere. Have the children take a photograph of their finished project and attach it in the Workbook.

Activity #2 Visit the Ark Encounter website.
Go to arkencounter.com. Explore this website and read explanations about the flood, the ark and Noah's family.

Ask: Which pages of this website were most interesting to you?

Have the children write about a page on this website that interested them.

Activity #3 Play the Freeze Game.

With this game, the children can learn to obey right away and completely. It is best to play it outside or in a large room. A leader will give directions to the players. These directions will be crazy commands like walk backward while holding your nose, or crab crawl on hands and feet. Then, when the leader wants the players to stop moving, he will say, "Freeze." Any player who moves after the Leader says, "Freeze" is out and must sit down. The last one playing is the most obedient and wins.

Activity #4 Which animals are "clean" and "unclean"?

MATERIALS NEEDED: A computer or telephone that has internet access

In **Genesis 7:2** God told Noah to bring on the ark seven pairs of every "clean" animal and only one pair of every animal that was not "clean." Have the children go to the website gotquestions.org to find out which animals were clean and unclean. Type in: "What made some animals clean and others unclean?" Have them list several clean and unclean animals in their Workbook.

Activity #5 Play the Coloring by Command game.

MATERIALS NEEDED: A set of crayons, coloring pencils or markers for the leader and each player, copies of the Lesson 4 Noah's ark coloring page

This game requires more than one player. One person is the leader and the others are players. Have the children turn to the Lesson 4 coloring picture of Noah's Ark at the back of the Workbook. The goal of this game is for players to follow all coloring commands given by the leader. One coloring command will be given at a time until the picture is completely colored. For example, the leader could say, "Color Noah's beard black," "Color the water blue" or "Color one monkey green and the other red." The leader will color her own copy following the same directions, so the players can compare their drawing to the leader's. The player with the higher number of "correct" colors wins.

Activity #6 Committing your whole life to God

Have the children write in their Workbook about what they think it would look like to commit their whole life to God.

ART PROJECTS

Project #1 Noah and the Ark Coloring Page

MATERIALS NEEDED: Crayons, coloring pencils or markers, Lesson 4 coloring page

Have the children color the Noah and the Ark coloring page in their Workbook.

Project #2 Make a Noah's ark mobile.

MATERIALS NEEDED: A wire hanger or two 18-inch wooden dowels tied together in a cross, string, Lesson 4 mobile patterns, scissors, crayons or markers, stapler

Have the children make a mobile of the ark and the animals from the Lesson 4 patterns in the Workbook. Have them trace and cut out the ark and animal patterns. The two halves of the ark will need to be stapled together. Color the patterns and staple a string to each one. Tie each string to the hanger or dowels. You might want to make the strings different lengths. Attach a string to the hanger or dowels, using it to hang the mobile from the ceiling or wall hook. Have your children take a photo of their mobiles and place it in their Workbook.

Project #3 Create a Noah's ark mural.

MATERIALS NEEDED: Butcher paper, pencils and markers

As a family or class, make a large mural of Noah and the ark.

Project #4 Paint a picture of the ark.

MATERIALS NEEDED: Watercolor paper, watercolors, brushes, jars of water and paper towels

Have the children make a watercolor painting of the ark and animals. Once their painting has dried, they could attach it in their Workbook.

Project #5 Make a traffic light.

MATERIALS NEEDED:
For the easy version—Red and green construction paper, a Popsicle stick, glue, the Lesson 4 circle pattern
For the more difficult version—Red, green and white construction paper, a paint stirring stick, crayons, glue, the Lesson 4 circle pattern

Have the children make a traffic light.

Say: We obey God for our own safety, just as we have to obey traffic lights and road signs for our safety.

a. Easy version – Using the circle pattern in the Workbook, trace and cut out one red and one green circle (the same size) out of construction paper and glue them on opposite sides of a Popsicle stick.

b. More difficult version – Cut a piece of white construction paper in half longwise (so that you have two tall and skinny pieces.) Glue these together with the paint stirring stick between them. Leave some stick exposed at the bottom so you can hold it up. Using the Lesson 4 circle pattern at the end of the Workbook, trace three 3-inch circles on each side in a line up and down. Use a crayon to color the red and yellow circles on one side, and the green and yellow circles on the other side. The correct order of the colors is red at the top, yellow in the middle, and green at the bottom. Using the circle pattern in the Workbook, trace and cut out one red circle from construction paper for one side and one green circle for the other side, and glue them on. These will seem brighter and easier to see than the other "lights" on the traffic light.

STUDY NOTES:

The following material is probably too advanced for most children, but we include these notes for you to decide about your child's comprehension level and for your personal learning.

Genesis 8:6-12

This passage in which Noah sends out and receives the dove serves as a symbol of God the Father and the Holy Spirit. The ARK represents THE DWELLING PLACE OF THE FATHER. NOAH might represent GOD THE FATHER, gently sending forth THE DOVE, THE HOLY SPIRIT, and then lovingly bringing back the dove into a place of rest, into His presence.

a. The first time Noah sent out the dove can be compared to when the Father sent His Spirit to people in the Old Testament. In those days, kings, priests and other individuals had an anointing of the Holy Spirit for a particular job. The Holy Spirit would come upon that person for a period of time, but then the Spirit would go back to the Father.

b. The second time Noah sent out the dove can be compared to when the Father sent the Holy Spirit to Jesus in the form of a dove at Jesus' baptism (**Luke 3:22**). In **Luke 4:1**, when Jesus was led into the desert, He is described as **"full of the Holy Spirit."** When Jesus walked the earth, He had the Holy Spirit in Him without measure. But when Jesus died, resurrected, and ascended into heaven He took the Spirit back with Him. Then the Father welcomed Jesus and the Holy Spirit back into His presence, just as Noah welcomed the dove carrying the olive leaf back into the ark. (The olive branch is a symbol of peace, and Jesus is known as the Prince of Peace in **Isaiah 9:6.**)

c.   After Jesus ascended into heaven He asked the Father to send the Spirit, the Comforter, to be with His disciples so that He would be with them and in them forever. The third time Noah sent out the dove can be compared to when the Father sent the Holy Spirit to be with Jesus' disciples. Like Jesus after His baptism, we can have the fullness of the Holy Spirit within us (**Ephesians 5:18**). Also, until Christ's second coming, the Holy Spirit will remain with us and in us, and not return to the Father.

LESSON 5

SPIRIT, SOUL, BODY— OUR DIFFERENT PARTS

OBJECTIVE

We hear God's voice in our spirit. So, we need to understand the difference between our spirit, soul and body.

SPIRIT, SOUL, BODY—OUR DIFFERENT PARTS

LESSON 5 CONTENT OBJECTIVE

To understand that we hear God's voice in our spirit. So, we need to understand the difference between our spirit, soul and body.

LESSON 5 KEY SCRIPTURE

Each day read aloud this lesson's scripture. Have the children write it out in the Workbook in the space provided. Encourage them to memorize this lesson's verse by the end of the week. Challenge the children to recite it without reading it.

1 Thessalonians 5:23 "…May he make you holy through and through. May your whole spirit, soul and body be kept free from blame…."

LESSON 5 READING ASSIGNMENT

Read Chapter 8 in *Is That Really You, God?*
Some children will need you to read portions of the assigned reading to them, others can read the chapters on their own or take turns reading aloud as a group.

TEACHING CONTENT, LEARNING ACTIVITIES AND ART PROJECTS

These are the largest components of the lesson. Depending upon your children's ages, you will need to decide how much of each section to cover in any given day. Select Learning Activities and Art Projects that fit your children's abilities and interests. Feel free to be creative and have fun as you lead your children into a real relationship with the Lord Jesus.

PRAYER AND MINISTRY TIME

Remember to choose a person who will receive prayer and ministry for this lesson. Help the children record this person's name in their Workbook. You should each agree to ask God to tell you something that will encourage that person. Refer to the prayer and ministry section of the Introduction, as needed.

Spirit, Soul and Body—What's the Difference?

Before teaching this lesson, you might want to familiarize yourself with the following terms:

Body = the house we live in, our physical body. The body communicates through our physical senses and appetites.

Soul = the part of us that holds our natural ability to perceive and feel. The soul is made up of the mind, will and emotions, so the soul communicates through our thoughts, intentions and feelings. The soul promotes *"self"*— *as in self-awareness, self-esteem* and *self-pity.* The characteristics of the soul can be either positive or negative.

In order to illustrate an abstract concept, we will say that the soul is located inside us in the area from the brain to the lower abdomen.

Spirit = the part of us that holds the life God placed in us when He created us. Our spirit is eternal and can respond to God. Our spirit is where the Holy Spirit comes to live when we accept Jesus as our Savior. The Holy Spirit communicates with us in our spirit.

For teaching purposes, we will say that the spirit is located inside us in the upper abdomen and lower chest.

Heart = a biblical term that can indicate a person's mind, will and emotions. However, the heart is also said to motivate and drive the mind, will and emotions. The redeemed heart is the dwelling place of Christ. So, one could say that the heart contains the spirit and the soul.

For more information on the spirit and soul, see the Study Notes at the end of this lesson. Here is a rough diagram of the body, soul and spirit.

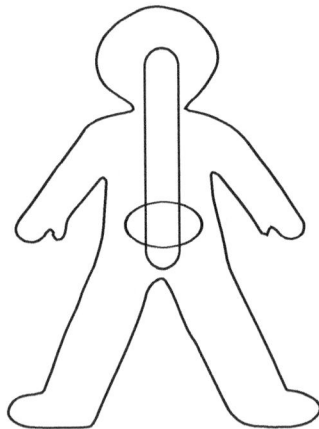

TEACHING CONTENT:

We are made up of different parts.

1. *Say:* God made us with many parts.

    Ask: Can you name some of the parts of your body?
    What about your insides? What is in there?

    Say: There are two other parts that God gave you that I want you to know about. They are also inside of you. Your SOUL (*move your hand from your brain to your lower abdomen*) and your SPIRIT (*place your hands over your upper abdomen and lower chest*).

    You remember from Lesson 1 that God made people in His image, to be like Him. Just as God is a three-part being—God the Father, Jesus the Son and the Holy Spirit, so we have three parts—our spirit, soul and body.

2. Help the children find and read aloud **1 Thessalonians 5:23.**
    "…May he make you holy through and through. May your whole spirit, soul and body be kept free from blame…."

    Say: Here God mentions our three parts that He wants us to keep holy—our spirit, soul and body.

    Using a large piece of paper on the floor, draw the outline of a person.

    Say: This shows your physical **BODY.** It is the house we live in. God gave each of us an amazing body that can do many things. Our body helps us learn about things as we see, smell, touch, hear and taste.

    Next, using a different color, draw an oblong around the area that includes the brain to the lower abdomen.

    Say: This next area shows our **SOUL.** The soul is made up of our **MIND,** our **WILL** and our **EMOTIONS.** The things that come from our soul—our thoughts, our decisions and our feelings—can be either helpful or hurtful.

    Then, using yet another color, draw a circle around the upper abdomen and lower chest.

    Say: This smaller circle shows our **SPIRIT.** Our spirit holds the life that God placed in us when He created us. Our spirit is eternal and can respond to God. Our spirit is where the Holy Spirit comes to live when we accept Jesus as our Savior. You could say: **I AM SPIRIT, I HAVE A SOUL AND I LIVE IN A BODY.**[1]

    ### LA #1, AP #1, AP #2, AP #3

3. *Say:* The Holy Spirit helps us by telling us in our spirit what God is saying. He often speaks quietly. We have to pay close attention so that we can hear Him.

    God speaks to us like a radio station. Just as a radio station is always sending a signal that your radio picks up, so the Lord is constantly speaking to us. Our spirit is the receiver of God's signals. But, many times our soul causes a problem—like a radio that has a lot of static noise because it is not exactly tuned to the station. The static from our soul can make it hard to hear God's voice clearly. We need to turn the dial from the soul to the spirit so that we can hear God clearly.

Here's an example: We might hear from God in our spirit that He wants us to talk to a person we don't know. He tells us to say something nice or to help them. But because we don't know that it is God telling us, we decide not to do it. Here, our soul (our thinking of why we shouldn't talk to someone we don't know) makes it hard to obey the Holy Spirit. Saying "No" to the Holy Spirit in our spirit makes us miss a chance to show God's love to that person. Obeying the Holy Spirit is easier when we RECOGNIZE that it is God's voice showing us what to do. We are learning to recognize God's voice.

Before we accept Jesus, our soul rules us. This may continue even after we accept Jesus because it is the only way we know. However, God wants His children to be ruled by the Holy Spirit in their spirit.

4. *Find and read aloud* **Ezekiel 36:26** and **Luke 6:45.**
Ezekiel 36:26 "I will give you new hearts. I will give you a new spirit that is faithful to me. I will remove your stubborn hearts from you. I will give you hearts that obey me."

Luke 6:45 "A good man says good things. These come from the good that is stored up in his heart. An evil man says evil things. These come from the evil that is stored up in his heart. A person's mouth says everything that is in their heart."

Say: Sometimes you will see the word HEART in the Bible. It can either mean the spirit or the soul, or both together.

We see in **Luke 6:45** above that the mouth and the heart are connected. What we speak shows what is in our heart.

5. *Find and read aloud* **James 3:9-10a.**
"With the tongue we praise our Lord and Father and with it we curse men, who have been made in God's likeness. Out of the same mouth come praise and cursing."

Say: Here's an example of that: You are driving in a car and are listening to music and worshiping God. Suddenly your brother or sister does something you don't like, and you get mad and scream at them. One minute you are praising God, the next moment you are cursing someone.

We have a choice to let the Holy Spirit fill our hearts so that the words that come out of our mouths are helpful.

Telling the difference between the spirit and soul

1. *Say*: Because we want to do only helpful things, we need to know if what we hear is from our soul or from our spirit. What we hear from the Holy Spirit in our spirit is always helpful. But what we hear from the soul could be helpful or hurtful.

Find and read aloud **Hebrews 4:12.**
"The word of God is alive and active. It is sharper than any sword that has two edges. It cuts deep enough to separate soul from spirit. It can separate bones from joints. It judges the thoughts and purposes of the heart."

Say: The sword mentioned here could be the sword used by a Roman soldier. It was a powerful weapon because it was sharp and good for cutting deep. This verse is saying that God's Word, the Bible, can help us tell the difference between the spirit and the soul. God's Word can help us know if what we hear is coming from our soul—our mind, will or emotions, or whether it is coming from God through our spirit. To be very clear, if what we hear does not agree with the Word of God, then it is not from God.

2. *Find and read aloud* **Deuteronomy 30:19-20a.**
   "I'm offering you the choice of life or death. You can choose either blessings or curses. But I want you to choose life. Then you and your children will live. And you will love the Lord your God. You will obey him. You will remain true to him. The Lord is your very life…."

Say: We have a choice to make. Do we let our soul rule us, or do we listen to the Holy Spirit in our spirit? In the next lesson we will learn how to let our spirit rule us and not our soul.

LA #2

PRAYER AND MINISTRY TIME:

Take turns sharing what the Lord has given you to share with the person receiving ministry. Allow time now to hear anything more that the Lord wants to say.

Review the Prayer and Ministry Time section of the Introduction, as needed.

LEARNING ACTIVITIES

Activity #1 The chocolate milk illustration

MATERIALS NEEDED: Tall clear glass, spoon, milk, chocolate syrup and a plate

Say: I am going to make a glass of chocolate milk to explain about our different parts and how God fits in our life. The glass is like our body. The milk is like our soul and spirit. *Place the glass on the plate and pour the milk into the glass.* Right now it is hard to see the difference between our soul and spirit.

When we ask Jesus into our lives, His Spirit comes to live inside our spirit. *Pour in the syrup.* The chocolate syrup is like the Holy Spirit in our spirit. But sometimes we don't pay attention to the Lord, and we live our life forgetting He is inside us. See how the chocolate settles to the bottom of the glass.

The spoon is like spending time reading the Word of God, or in prayer and worship. *Pick up the spoon and stir.* When we spend time with God by reading the Bible, talking to Him in prayer, or worshiping Him, we allow the Holy Spirit to "flavor" our soul.

Ask: Can you tell where only the milk is now?
   Can you see only the chocolate?
   [No, they are mixed together so that they are one.]

Say: When we spend time with God, we become one with Him. People can't tell where we stop and where the Holy Spirit begins—we are together.

Allow the chocolate milk to sit and separate. During this time, let the children make their own glass of chocolate milk. After the children have a glass of milk, go back to the teacher's glass and have the children look at it now.

Say: Look! The milk and chocolate have separated. If we don't spend time with God by reading His Word, talking to Him in prayer, or worshiping Him (*lay the spoon down next to the milk*), we separate and pretty soon people don't

SEE Jesus in us anymore. *Pick up the spoon and stir the syrup again.* But if we begin to pray to God, read His Word, and worship Him, soon we will be more like Jesus again.

Begin stirring vigorously, so that some milk flows out over the top of the glass. Say: In fact, if we spend enough time receiving God's love, we will be a blessing to other people as God's love spills out from our lives to others.

Summary: It is important for us to allow our spirit, where the Holy Spirit lives, to be stirred up inside of us so that other people see Jesus when they look at us. The Holy Spirit flavors our thoughts, our feelings, our decisions, how we use our body, and how we feel about God. The Holy Spirit makes our spirit, soul and body holy. He helps our spirit to hear God, so God can guide us, teach us and tell us how much He loves us and others.

Activity #2 A matching challenge
Have the children turn to their Workbook and draw lines from each word on the left to what describes it on the right:

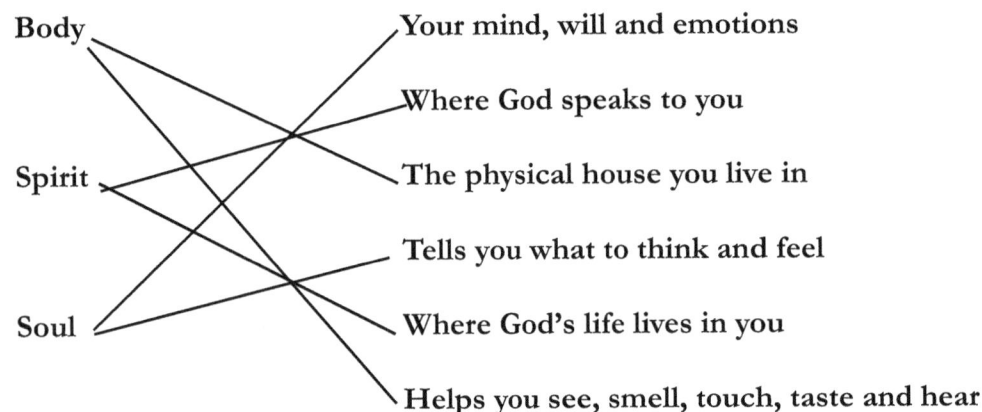

Body	Your mind, will and emotions
	Where God speaks to you
Spirit	The physical house you live in
	Tells you what to think and feel
Soul	Where God's life lives in you
	Helps you see, smell, touch, taste and hear

ART PROJECTS

Project #1 Make a play-dough body, soul and spirit
MATERIALS NEEDED: Three colors of play-dough, gingerbread man cookie cutter

Using a cookie cutter, have the children make a play-dough gingerbread man. Shape a soul and spirit from different colored play-dough, to look like the Lesson 5 patterns for the soul and spirit at the back of the Workbook. Discuss what is in the spirit, soul and body.

Project #2 Sidewalk chalk spirit, soul and body
MATERIALS NEEDED: Three colors of sidewalk chalk

Have the children lay down on a driveway or sidewalk. Trace around each child's body with sidewalk chalk. Ask the children to draw in where the soul and spirit are with different colors of chalk. Label each part: spirit, soul and body. Discuss what each of these represent.

Project #3 The spirit, soul and body on paper
MATERIALS NEEDED: Lesson 5 spirit, soul and body patterns, paper, scissors, glue, crayons or pencils

Make a paper person showing the body, soul and spirit. Help the children trace the patterns in the Workbook of the body, soul and spirit onto paper and cut out these shapes. Have them glue the soul and spirit on the body and label each part: body, soul and spirit. Discuss what each represents.

STUDY NOTES:

Here is additional information about the terms spirit, soul, body and heart.

Body – *Sarx* in Greek is the house we live in, our physical body. The body communicates through our physical senses and appetites. It can be called the outer man or carnal man. When we die our physical bodies decay, but God gives us spiritual bodies after death[2] (see **1 Corinthians 15:44; Matthew 10:28**).

Soul – *Psuche* (psoo-khay´) in Greek is the part of us that holds our natural ability to perceive and feel. The soul is comprised of the mind, will and emotions, so the soul communicates through our thoughts, intentions and feelings. The soul promotes "self"—as in self-awareness, self-esteem and self-pity. The characteristics of the soul can be either positive or negative. The soul is eternal[3] (see **Matthew 10:28, Acts 2:27**).

Spirit – *Pneuma* (pnyoo´-mah) in Greek is the part of us where God's life lives. When we believe in Jesus as our Savior, the Holy Spirit indwells us and communicates with our spirit. Our spirit is the part of us that can fully respond to God. Our spirit is eternal[4] (see **Hebrews 12:23; 1 Peter 3:19**).

Heart – *Kardia* (kar-dee´-ah) in Greek is the core of an individual. According to Eerdmans Bible Dictionary, this term can indicate a person's mind, will and emotions, and the heart is also said to motivate and drive the mind, will and emotions. The redeemed heart is the dwelling place of Christ.[5] So, one could say that the heart contains the spirit and the soul.

LESSON 6

SPIRIT, SOUL, BODY—
WHO RULES?

OBJECTIVE

*Because we hear God's voice in our spirit,
we need to allow our spirit to rule us.*

SPIRIT, SOUL AND BODY—WHO RULES?

LESSON 6 CONTENT OBJECTIVE

To understand that because we hear God's voice in our spirit, we need to allow our spirit to rule us.

LESSON 6 KEY SCRIPTURE

Each day read aloud this lesson's scripture. Have the children write it out in the Workbook in the space provided. Encourage them to memorize this lesson's verse by the end of the week. Challenge the children to recite it without reading it.

Matthew 11:28-30 "Come to me, all you who are tired and are carrying heavy loads. I will give you rest. Become my servants and learn from me…Serving me is easy, and my load is light."

LESSON 6 READING ASSIGNMENT

Read Chapter 9 in *Is That Really You, God?*
Some children will need you to read portions of the assigned reading to them, others can read the chapters on their own or take turns reading aloud as a group.

TEACHING CONTENT, LEARNING ACTIVITIES AND ART PROJECTS

These are the largest components of the lesson. Depending upon your children's ages, you will need to decide how much of each section to cover in any given day. Select Learning Activities and Art Projects that fit your children's abilities and interests. Feel free to be creative and have fun as you lead your children into a real relationship with the Lord Jesus.

PRAYER AND MINISTRY TIME

Remember to choose a person who will receive prayer and ministry for this lesson. Help the children record this person's name in their Workbook. You should each agree to ask God to tell you something that will encourage that person. Refer to the prayer and ministry section of the Introduction, as needed.

Spirit, Soul and Body—Who Rules?

TEACHING CONTENT

We either obey our spirit or our soul.

1. *Say*: In this lesson we will learn how to let our spirit rule us. We don't want our soul to rule us because what we hear from our soul is not always from God. We are born a natural human being. We come into this world and our soul rules us. Our mind, will and emotions are our guides. We do whatever feels good or seems right to us. After we invite Jesus into our life, our spirit becomes born again. God's Holy Spirit then lives inside us to help us become like Jesus. God uses the Bible to show us how Jesus thinks and wants us to act.

    Our thoughts and actions can be ruled by either our soul or by our spirit, where God speaks to us. Remember, Noah did not let questions, doubts or feelings keep him from obeying what he heard God say in his spirit. Noah let his spirit rule him and not his soul—his mind, will or emotions.

2. *Help the children find and read aloud* **James 3:13-16.**
    Is anyone among you wise and understanding? That person should show it by living a good life. A wise person isn't proud when they do good deeds. But suppose your hearts are jealous and bitter. Suppose you are concerned only about getting ahead. Then don't brag about it. And don't say no to the truth. Wisdom like this doesn't come down from heaven. It belongs to the earth. It doesn't come from the Holy Spirit. It comes from the devil. Are you jealous? Are you concerned only about getting ahead? Then your life will be a mess. You will be doing all kinds of evil things.

    Say: These verses show what it can be like to be ruled by our soul. We can be proud and brag about good things we do. We can be jealous or bitter, wanting to be better than others. We can refuse to listen to the truth.

3. *Find and read aloud* **James 3:17-18.**
    But the wisdom that comes from heaven is pure. That's the most important thing about it. And that's not all. It also loves peace. It thinks about others. It obeys. It is full of mercy and good fruit. It is fair. It doesn't pretend to be what it is not. Those who make peace plant it like a seed. They will harvest a crop of right living.

    Say: The **"wisdom that comes from heaven"** is what the Holy Spirit speaks in our spirit.

    Ask: According to these verses, what happens when our spirit rules us?
    [The Holy Spirit in our spirit will always help us be pure, peacemakers, thoughtful towards others, obedient, merciful, fair and honest.]

4. *Find and read aloud* **1 Corinthians 2:7-16.**
    Say: When we are ruled by the soul, we can be like a person without the Spirit in **verse 14.** Spiritual things may seem foolish to our own mind. But when our spirit rules us, we can have God's wisdom. The Holy Spirit in us knows what God thinks, and He can give us the mind of Christ so that we understand what to say or do.

    LA #1, LA #2

Let's fine-tune our spirit and get rid of the static from our soul.

Say: So, here's how we tune-in to what our spirit is saying and tune-out what our soul is saying.

1. With God's Word—
Find and read aloud **James 1:21: "So get rid of everything that is sinful. Get rid of the evil that is all around us. Don't be too proud to accept the word that is planted in you. It can save you."**

Say: **"The word that is planted in you"** is the scripture we hear and read. Normally, our MIND likes to figure out what to do in a situation. Our thinking can go back and forth about it, not sure of what to do. As we read the Bible, the Holy Spirit can give us wisdom and bring our mind into line with God's thoughts.

2. With Prayer—
Find and read aloud **Matthew 26:36-46.**

> **Then Jesus went with his disciples to a place called Gethsemane. He said to them, "Sit here while I go over there and pray." He took Peter and the two sons of Zebedee along with him. He began to be sad and troubled. Then he said to them, "My soul is very sad. I feel close to death. Stay here. Keep watch with me."**
>
> **He went a little farther. Then he fell with his face to the ground. He prayed, "My Father, if it is possible, take this cup of suffering away from me. But let what you want be done, not what I want."**
>
> **Then he returned to his disciples and found them sleeping. "Couldn't you men keep watch with me for one hour?" he asked Peter. "Watch and pray. Then you won't fall into sin when you are tempted. The spirit is willing, but the body is weak."**
>
> **Jesus went away a second time. He prayed, "My Father, is it possible for this cup to be taken away? But if I must drink it, may what you want be done."**
>
> **Then he came back. Again he found them sleeping. They couldn't keep their eyes open. So he left them and went away once more. For the third time he prayed the same thing.**
>
> **Then he returned to the disciples. He said to them, "Are you still sleeping and resting? Look! The hour has come. The Son of Man is about to be handed over to sinners. Get up! Let us go! Here comes the one who is handing me over to them!"**

Re-read **verses 38-39.**

Say: In the Garden of Gethsemane, Jesus' soul was filled with sadness, and He did not WANT to do what He knew the Father wanted. Sometimes our soul fights against what God is asking us to do. Jesus understood the fight between the soul and spirit. He kept praying (three times) until He won and was ready to obey.

Sometimes our will can be very strong and work against what God wants. Our will can make a plan that is not God's plan, or it can be impatient and not wait for God's right time. Prayer is the answer when our will is out of line with God's will. If we find our delight in God and spend time with Him, His desires become our desires (**Psalm 37:4-6**). If we stay connected with God by praying and thinking about what He says in the Bible, we will be able to patiently wait for God to do it in His own time and way (**John 15:7**).

AP #1, AP #2

3. With Praise—
Find and read aloud **Psalm 57:6-11.**

> **My enemies spread a net to catch me by the feet.**
> > **I felt helpless.**

> They dug a pit in my path.
> > But they fell into it themselves.
> God, my heart feels secure.
> > My heart feels secure.
> > I will sing and make music to you.
> My spirit, wake up! (In the NIV it says, "Awake my soul!")
> > Harp and lyre, wake up!
> > I want to sing and make music before the sun rises.
> Lord, I will praise you among the nations.
> > I will sing about you among the people of the earth.
> Great is your love. It reaches to the heavens.
> > Your truth reaches to the skies.
> God, may you be honored above the heavens.
> > Let your glory be over all the earth.

Say: The psalm writer's soul felt helpless and discouraged, but he chose to praise God. At first he may not have felt like praising, but He **CHOSE** to praise God anyway. Sometimes we need to make a sacrifice of praise—we give up what we want to do, like feeling sorry for ourselves, and choose to praise God. Praise helps us remember how great God is and helps us forget about our problems. For example, thanking God is the best way to stop feeling sorry for ourselves.

4. *Find and read aloud* **Psalm 42:5** *in* The Message *version of the Bible.*
"**Why are you down in the dumps, dear soul? Why are you crying the blues? Fix my eyes on God—soon I'll be praising again. He puts a smile on my face. He's my God.**"

Say: Our **EMOTIONS** are changed by how things are going. If things are going the way we want, we feel happy. If things are not going our way, we feel sad or angry. Spending time praising God will help us remember that He is in control and He loves us.

LA #3

5. *Say:* So, here is what we can do when our soul wants to rule us:
   - If your **MIND** wants you to think hurtful thoughts, spend time **READING THE BIBLE**, God's Word.
   - If your **WILL** wants you to do something you shouldn't, spend time **PRAYING**—talking and listening to God.
   - If your **EMOTIONS** are stuck in a hurtful feeling like jealousy, anger or feeling sorry for yourself, spend time **PRAISING GOD**.

Moving from being led by the soul to being led by the spirit is like shifting your weight from one foot to the other while skiing or skateboarding. The motion is small, but it makes a big difference in what happens.

LA #4

6. *Find and read aloud* **Matthew 11:28-30.**
"**Come to me, all you who are tired and are carrying heavy loads. I will give you rest. Become my servants and learn from me. I am gentle and free of pride. You will find rest for your souls. Serving me is easy, and my load is light.**"

Say: When we are being led by our soul, we will feel tired, like we are carrying a heavy load. When we are led by the Holy Spirit in our spirit, we will be gentle and humble, and find rest for our mind, will and emotions.

When our will is leading—when we insist on OUR way—it feels like we are pushing. We need to be careful because Satan can affect how we think, feel and what we want to do. Satan pushes; the Holy Spirit leads.

7. *Find and read aloud* **Galatians 5:25.**
   "Since we live by the Spirit, let us keep in step with the Spirit."

   Say: Let's choose to listen to the Holy Spirit in our spirit and follow Him.

   AP #3

PRAYER AND MINISTRY TIME:

Take turns sharing what the Lord has given you to say to the person receiving ministry. Allow time now to hear anything more that the Lord wants to say.

Review the Prayer and Ministry Time section of the Introduction, as needed.

LEARNING ACTIVITIES

Activity #1 Draw a life-size body, soul and spirit.

MATERIALS NEEDED: Butcher block paper, crayons or magic markers

Have the children lay down on a large piece of paper. Trace around each child's body. Let the children draw in his face, hair, fingers and toes, etc. Have the children draw where the spirit and soul would be on the picture of their body.

Alternatively, if you live near a beach, you could have your child lay down on the sand. Trace around your child's body with your finger or a stick.

Or if it snows, you could have your child lay down on the ground. Trace around your child's body in the snow with a stick.

Ask: What is in your spirit?
   [It has the life that God placed in us. The Holy Spirit is in our spirit if we have accepted Jesus as our Savior.]

Ask: What might the Holy Spirit say in your spirit?
   [He shows us what to do. He tells us that God loves us.]

Say: Remember, our soul is made up of our mind, will and emotions.

Ask: Our mind thinks. What is an example of what we think about?
   [An example is, "I think about what I want for my birthday."]

Ask: Our will decides. What is an example of what we decide?
   [An example is, "I decide to share my magic markers."]

Ask: Our emotions cause feelings. What is an example of how we feel?
[An example is, "I feel rejected when a friend leaves me to play with someone else."
Guide the children to express both positive and negative characteristics of the soul.]

Say: The soul can have either a positive or negative influence on us.

Ask: What might happen if we allowed our negative feelings to rule us?
[One example is, if a friend left you to play with someone else, you might feel so rejected and angry that you do something mean towards your younger sister.]

Ask: What could the Holy Spirit say to us in our spirit about being rejected by a friend?
   How could the Holy Spirit help us deal with feeling rejected?
   What could God say to us when we feel rejected and angry?
[The Holy Spirit might say that even though that friend rejected me, God accepts me and loves me. He will help me be kind to that friend and make other friends.]

Activity #2 Make a spirit, soul and body gingerbread cookie.
MATERIALS NEEDED: Gingerbread dough—either pre-made or from scratch, gingerbread man cookie cutter, icing with a nozzle, candy heart or chocolate chip.

Have the children make a real gingerbread man out of cookie dough. Bake in the oven and then let the gingerbread man cool. Using a container of icing with a nozzle, draw the outline of the soul on the cookie. Include the head, the chest and the stomach (the mind, will and emotions). With icing, glue a red candy or chocolate chip on the gingerbread man's upper abdomen where the spirit is.

While the gingerbread man is baking, review what it is like to be ruled by the spirit and what it is like to be ruled by the soul. Then ask the children to write about what it is like for them to be ruled by the spirit and by the soul, respectively.

Activity #3 Why so downcast, oh my soul?
MATERIALS NEEDED: A phone or computer with internet access

Search YouTube for the song "Acapella Praise – Why so downcast, oh my soul." Have the children listen to the song and see how we can use praise music when we are stuck in feelings of worry or sadness.

Say: Praising God reminds us that He is good and strong, and He loves us.

Have the children write in their Workbook the name of a praise song that helps them stop feeling worried or sad. Have them write out what that song says about God.

Activity #4 Let your spirit rule you.
Review the suggestions in this lesson for letting our spirit rule us:

- If your **MIND** wants you to think hurtful thoughts, spend time **READING THE BIBLE**, God's Word.
- If your **WILL** wants you to do something you shouldn't, spend time **PRAYING**—talking and listening to God.
- If your **EMOTIONS** are stuck in a hurtful feeling like jealousy, anger or feeling sorry for yourself, spend time **PRAISING GOD**.

Encourage the children to keep their eyes open for a time this week when they need to let their spirit rule them, not their soul. Encourage them to use God's Word, prayer to God or praising God to rule their mind, will and emotions. Have them write about that situation in the Workbook.

ART PROJECTS

Project #1 Draw Jesus in the Garden of Gethsemane.
MATERIALS NEEDED: Markers, crayons or colored pencils

Have the children read **Matthew 26:36-46** again. Have them draw a picture in the Workbook of Jesus praying in the Garden of Gethsemane.

Project #2 The Disciples find Jesus Praying coloring page
MATERIALS NEEDED: Markers, crayons or colored pencils

Have the children color in the coloring page The Disciples Find Jesus Praying in their Workbook.

Project #3 Draw Jesus lightening your load.
MATERIALS NEEDED: Markers, crayons or colored pencils

Have the children read **Matthew 11:28-30** again. Have them draw a picture in the Workbook of what it might look like to have Jesus give you rest by giving you a light load to carry instead of a heavy load.

LESSON 7

GOD WILL HELP US

OBJECTIVE

We should ask God for help when we feel weak, afraid or are in trouble.

GOD WILL HELP US

LESSON 7 CONTENT OBJECTIVE
To understand that we should ask God for help when we feel weak, afraid or are in trouble.

LESSON 7 KEY SCRIPTURES:
Each day read aloud this lesson's scriptures. Have the children write them out in the Workbook in the space provided. Encourage them to memorize one of this lesson's verses by the end of the week. Challenge them to recite it without reading it.

2 Chronicles 20:4 "The people came together to ask the LORD for help. In fact, they came from every town in Judah to pray to him."

Jeremiah 33:3 "Call out to me. I will answer you. I will tell you great things you do not know...."

LESSON 7 READING ASSIGNMENT
Read Chapter 10 in *Is That Really You, God?*
Some children will need you to read portions of the assigned reading to them, others can read the chapters on their own or take turns reading aloud as a group.

TEACHING CONTENT, LEARNING ACTIVITIES AND ART PROJECTS
These are the largest components of the lesson. Depending upon your children's ages, you will need to decide how much of each section to cover in any given day. Select Learning Activities and Art Projects that fit your children's abilities and interests. Feel free to be creative and have fun as you lead your children into a real relationship with the Lord Jesus.

PRAYER AND MINISTRY TIME:
Remember to choose a person who will receive prayer and ministry for this lesson. Help the children record this person's name in their Workbook. You should each agree to ask God to tell you something that will encourage that person. Refer to the prayer and ministry section of the Introduction, as needed.

God Will Help Us

TEACHING CONTENT

What happened before 2 Chronicles 19 and 20?

1. *Say*: Today we are going to learn about Jehoshaphat, the King of Judah. He was a king who loved the Lord and always tried to obey Him. Jehoshaphat stopped all his people from worshiping false gods, and encouraged them to worship the LORD. God was pleased with King Jehoshaphat, and King Jehoshaphat loved the Lord (**2 Chronicles 17:3-6**). But he forgot something a prophet had told his father, who had been king before him. It was a warning from God.

   Help the children find and read aloud **2 Chronicles 15:2b.**
   "The LORD is with you when you are with him. If you really look for him, you will find him. But if you desert him, he will desert you."

   Say: The prophet was saying that when we forget about God and don't try to hear His voice, we are still His children, but our friendship with Him is hurt. We won't hear when He wants to tell us something.

2. *Say*: Then Jehoshaphat made a big mistake. He let his soul rule him. He decided to go to war with the wicked King of Israel, even though a prophet of God warned them that it would not go well. It turns out that Jehoshaphat was almost killed in the battle. Thankfully, he called out to God for help (**2 Chronicles 18:31-32**).

   Ask: Do you remember a time when you knew you weren't supposed to do something, but you went ahead and did it?

Jehoshaphat learned from his mistake.

1. *Say*: Jehoshaphat did not want to make that mistake again. He loved God with all his heart and decided to listen to what God had to say. He encouraged the leaders and all the people in his land to love God and listen to Him (**2 Chronicles 19:1-11**).

2. *Say*: One day, some of the nearby nations decided to go to war against Jehoshaphat and his people in Judah.

   Find and read aloud **2 Chronicles 20:1-2.**
   > **After that, the Moabites, Ammonites and some Meunites went to war against Jehoshaphat. Some people came and told him, "A huge army is coming from Edom to fight against you. They have come across the Dead Sea. They are already in Hazezon Tamar." Hazezon Tamar is also called En Gedi.**

   Ask: How would you feel if you heard that a huge army was coming to fight against you?
   [Most people would want to run the other way!]

   Say: King Jehoshaphat was afraid when he heard this news, but he decided he HAD to know what God wanted him to do.

3. *Find and read aloud* **2 Chronicles 20:3-4.**
"Jehoshaphat was alarmed. So he decided to ask the Lord for advice. He told all the people of Judah to go without eating. The people came together to ask the Lord for help. In fact, they came from every town in Judah to pray to him."

Say: When you pray and fast, it shows that you really want God's help. A fast usually refers to going without food while you pray and listen to God. We do not recommend that children do this. Instead, some families choose to fast from sugar, soda, electronics or another form of entertainment. However, in this passage, all the Israelites went without food while they were praying and waiting on God.

4. *Find and read aloud* **2 Chronicles 20:6-12.**
Say: So, Jehoshaphat called all the people of Israel together to pray, and this was his prayer to God. Basically, He prayed, "Lord God, You are King of all the earth. You are strong and mighty. No one is like You! You gave us this land. We are Your people, and now our enemies come to fight us. We don't know what to do. We look to You to hear us and save us."

Jehoshaphat and the people asked God for help before doing anything else. King Jehoshaphat's prayer was honest and humble. He admitted that he didn't know what to do, and he needed God's help. He remembered how powerful the LORD is and how much God cares for His people.

5. *Find and read aloud* **2 Chronicles 20:13.**
"All the men of Judah stood there in front of the LORD. Their wives, children and little ones were with them."

Say: Then Jehoshaphat and the people waited on God for an answer.

Ask: Was there a time when you were not sure what to do and you asked God for help?
Did you have to wait a while before you knew what to do?

God gives the answer.

1. *Find and read aloud* **2 Chronicles 20:14-17.**
Then the Spirit of the Lord came on Jahaziel. He was standing among the people of Israel...Jahaziel said, "King Jehoshaphat, listen! All you who live in Judah and Jerusalem, listen! The Lord says to you, 'Do not be afraid. Do not lose hope because of this huge army. The battle is not yours. It is God's. Tomorrow march down against them. They will be climbing up by the Pass of Ziz. You will find them at the end of the valley in the Desert of Jeruel. You will not have to fight this battle. Take your positions. Stand firm. You will see how the Lord will save you. Judah and Jerusalem, do not be afraid. Do not lose hope. Go out and face them tomorrow. The Lord will be with you.'"

Say: God spoke through a prophet named Jahaziel. Jehoshaphat listened to what the Holy Spirit was saying through this prophet.

Ask: How would you have felt if you had been fasting and praying, and then you heard this prophecy?

LA #1

2. *Find and read aloud* **2 Chronicles 20:18-19.**
"**Jehoshaphat bowed down with his face toward the ground. All the people of Judah and Jerusalem also bowed down. They worshiped the Lord. Then some Levites from the families of Kohath and Korah stood up. They praised the Lord, the God of Israel. They praised him with very loud voices.**"

Say: Jehoshaphat and his people decided to believe this great news! They were so grateful to God for promising that He would be with them, and that they would not have to fight this battle. They worshiped God.

King Jehoshaphat obeyed.

1. *Find and read aloud again* **2 Chronicles 20:16.**
"**Tomorrow march down against them….**"

Say: This is what the Lord had told them to do. So King Jehoshaphat obeyed what God had said, and he waited to move until God's set time.

2. *Find and read aloud* **2 Chronicles 20:20–21.**
"**Early in the morning all the people left for the Desert of Tekoa. As they started out, Jehoshaphat stood up. He said, "Judah, listen to me! People of Jerusalem, listen to me! Have faith in the Lord your God. He'll take good care of you. Have faith in his prophets. Then you will have success." Jehoshaphat asked the people for advice. Then he appointed men to sing to the Lord. He wanted them to praise the Lord because of his glory and holiness. They marched out in front of the army. They said,**
"**Give thanks to the Lord. His faithful love continues forever.**"

Say: Jehoshaphat stood up and talked to his people. He did not want them to be afraid or lose hope, but instead to obey God. Jehoshaphat encouraged his people to have faith in God and believe what the Holy Spirit said through the prophet. We need to have faith when we hear from the Holy Spirit. We can believe that if we obey God's directions, God will do what He says He will do.

The results of obeying God's direction

1. **Verse 22** *in the NIrV is confusing. Instead, read aloud from the NIV.*
"**As they began to sing and praise, the Lord set ambushes against the men of Ammon and Moab and Mount Seir who were invading Judah, and they were defeated**" (NIV).

Find and read aloud **2 Chronicles 20:23-24** *in the NIrV.*
"**The Ammonites and Moabites rose up against the men from Mount Seir. They destroyed them. They put an end to them. When they finished killing the men from Seir, they destroyed one another.**
The men of Judah came to the place that looks out over the desert. They turned to look down at the huge army. But all they saw was dead bodies lying there on the ground. No one had escaped."

Say: It turns out that when the people of Judah sang praises to the LORD and expected Him to fight for them, God began to defeat their enemies. When the people got to the battlefield, the battle was already over! When we obey God's directions, we can count on Him working things out.

2. *Find and read aloud* **2 Chronicles 20:25.**
"So Jehoshaphat and his men went down there to carry off anything of value. Among the dead bodies they found a large amount of supplies, clothes and other things of value. There was more than they could take away. There was so much it took three days to collect all of it."

Ask: Can you imagine how happy the people were?

3. *Find and read aloud* **2 Chronicles 20:26-28.**
On the fourth day they gathered together in the Valley of Berakah. There they praised the Lord. That's why it's called the Valley of Berakah to this day.
Then all the men of Judah and Jerusalem returned to Jerusalem. They were filled with joy. Jehoshaphat led them. The Lord had made them happy because all their enemies were dead. They entered Jerusalem and went to the Lord's temple. They were playing harps, lyres and trumpets.

Say: First they gathered in the Valley of Berakah to praise God, and then they went back to Jerusalem where they praised and worshiped God again! The people gave God all the credit and glory for this victory.

4. *Find and read aloud* **2 Chronicles 20:29-30**.
"All the surrounding kingdoms began to have respect for God. They had heard how the Lord had fought against Israel's enemies. The kingdom of Jehoshaphat was at peace. His God had given him peace and rest on every side."

Say: The nations all around Judah had great respect for the Lord because of what He had done for Jehoshaphat and his people. Because of Jehoshaphat's obedience and what God did, the people in Judah had joy, peace and rest.

Ask: Have you ever sensed God telling you to do something and you obeyed?
What happened when you obeyed?
Did you have joy, peace or rest?

LA #2, AP #1, AP #2, AP #3

Review
As the children are enjoying a snack, talk about today's lesson.

1. *Say:* Jehoshaphat was the king of Judah.

Ask: What is it like to be a king?
[When you are a king, you are in charge. If you are a good king, you tell people what they need to do for the good of the whole kingdom.]

Ask: Jehoshaphat could have made up his own plan to fight the enemy, but what did he do?
[He asked God and listened to Him. Jehoshaphat obeyed God and let Him be his King!]

2. *To review the spirit, soul, and body concepts from the previous weeks' lessons, draw on a piece of paper the body, soul and spirit diagram used in Lesson 5.*

Point to the spirit and say: This is our spirit where the Holy Spirit speaks to us. *Draw a cross inside the spirit.*

Point to the soul and say: This is our soul where we think, feel and decide. *Draw a stick figure of a man inside the soul to represent our own mind, will and emotions.*

Ask: When the large armies came to attack Jehoshaphat in **2 Chronicles 20**, did he let his soul or his spirit guide him?
　[Jehoshaphat listened to what God said to do and obeyed Him. He followed the Holy Spirit instead of doing his own thing and being ruled by his soul.]

Ask: What could have happened if Jehoshaphat had made up his own plan?
　[Without God's help, all his people probably would have been killed.]

Say: In the next lesson we will learn about a king who DECIDED to follow his OWN plan.

LA #3, LA #4, AP #4, AP #5

PRAYER AND MINISTRY TIME
Take turns sharing what the Lord has given you to share with the person receiving ministry. Allow time now to hear anything more that the Lord wants to say.

Review the Prayer and Ministry Time section of the Introduction, as needed.

LEARNING ACTIVITIES

Activity #1 The Holy Spirit helps us.
MATERIALS NEEDED: A Bible

In Old Testament times, God placed the Holy Spirit on a few special people like kings, prophets, priests or judges. To hear from God, people had to wait until He spoke through a prophet. But after Jesus died on the cross, rose from the dead and returned to heaven, God sent the Holy Spirit to live in anyone who believes in Jesus! Although God can still speak through a prophet, we average people can hear directly from God through His Holy Spirit.

Have the children read **John 14:16-17; John 14:26** and **John 16:13-14**, and then list in the Workbook what the Holy Spirit wants to do for them.

Activity #2 Praise God for what He has done for you.
MATERIALS NEEDED: Musical instruments, a recording of a praise song that describes God's goodness and power

Have the children list in their Workbook some of the things that God has done for them. Gather any musical instruments you have. Join them as they play instruments and sing along with a praise song, thanking God for what He has done. Encourage them to worship God in their heart, telling God how much they love Him.

A possible choice would be "Shout to the Lord" by Darlene Zschech. Search YouTube for the song with lyrics. You could type in "SHOUT TO THE LORD (LYRICS)" by Ale Quintana.

Activity #3 Act out King Jehoshaphat's battle.
MATERIALS NEEDED: King's crown, soldiers' swords, musical instruments, a computer or telephone with internet

access or a recording of a praise song that describes God's goodness and power.
Have the children re-enact the story of King Jehoshaphat's defeat of Ammon, Moab and Mount Seir in **2 Chronicles 20**, using props or costumes. Use a recoding of a favorite praise song or Search YouTube for a praise song that speaks of God's goodness and power. As you march into battle, sing or play musical instruments along with this song. Have the children write in their Workbook the name of the song they used to praise God.

A possible choice would be "Shout to the Lord" by Darlene Zschech. Search YouTube for the song with lyrics. You could type in "SHOUT TO THE LORD (LYRICS)" by Ale Quintana.

Activity #4 Watch videos about 2 Chronicles 20
MATERIALS NEEDED: A phone or computer with internet access

Search YouTube for these videos and watch them:
• Sunday School Lesson for Kids - Give Thanks to the Lord - 2 Chronicles 20 Sharefaithkids
• Awaken Dance / Jehoshaphat

ART PROJECTS

Project #1 Make a drum.
MATERIALS NEEDED: An oatmeal container, wrapping paper, scissors and glue

Have the children make a drum. Tape the top of an oatmeal container onto the container. Glue on decorative wrapping paper. Show the children how to tap the top of the drum with their fingers or a wooden spoon.

Project #2 Make a jingler.
MATERIALS NEEDED: Plastic or paper cup, hammer and nail, yarn, Scotch tape, scissors and jingle bells

Have the children make a jingler. Tie jingle bells onto pieces of yarn. Punch holes in the bottom of the cup with a hammer and nail. Thread the yarn through the holes, knot the yarn, and secure with tape. With the cup upside down, the jingle bells should hang inside of the cup. Show the children how to shake the cup, holding the narrow end.

Project #3 Make a tambourine.
MATERIALS NEEDED: Two aluminum pie pans, jingle bells, colorful electrical tape, colorful fabric and scissors

Have the children make a tambourine. Cut colorful fabric streamers and tape them into one pie pan, so that they hang down from it. Place jingle bells inside of one pan, and tape a second pie pan on top of it. Show the children how to hold the tambourine with the streamers hanging down. Have them gently, but sharply, strike the flat side of the tambourine with their hand, making the bells jingle inside.

Project #4 Draw a picture from 2 Chronicles 20.
MATERIALS NEEDED: Markers, crayons or colored pencils

Have the children draw a picture in the Workbook of one of the scenes from **2 Chronicles 20:1-28**. This could be:
• When Jehoshaphat, the men, women and children of Judah fasted and prayed to the Lord for help, and then Jahaziel heard from God.
• When the people of Judah marched out to meet the enemy, singing and praising God.

- When they looked out over the battle field and saw that their enemies were already dead.

Project #5 Jehoshaphat and the People of Judah Praying coloring page

MATERIALS NEEDED: Markers, crayons or colored pencils

Have the children color in the Lesson 7 coloring page in the Workbook that shows Jehoshaphat and the people of Judah praying.

LESSON 8

OBEYING GOD IS BEST

OBJECTIVE

There are obstacles that get in the way of our hearing and obeying God's voice. When we remove them, we will be able to listen and obey. Obeying God is always best for us.

OBEYING GOD IS BEST

LESSON 8 CONTENT OBJECTIVE

To understand that some things make it harder for us to hear and obey God's voice. When we recognize what gets in the way of hearing God's voice, it helps us choose to listen and obey. Obeying God is always best for us.

LESSON 8 KEY SCRIPTURES

Each day read aloud this lesson's scriptures. Have the children write them out in the Workbook in the space provided. Encourage the children to memorize one of this lesson's verses by the end of the week. Challenge them to recite it without reading it.

1 Samuel 15:22 "What pleases the Lord more?…It is better to obey than to offer a sacrifice."

1 John 1:9 "…If we admit that we have sinned, he will forgive us our sins. He will forgive every wrong thing we have done. He will make us pure."

LESSON 8 READING ASSIGNMENT

Read Chapters 11 and 12 in *Is That Really You, God?*
Some children will need you to read portions of the assigned reading to them, others can read the chapters on their own or take turns reading aloud as a group.

TEACHING CONTENT, LEARNING ACTIVITIES AND ART PROJECTS

These are the largest components of the lesson. Depending upon your children's ages, you will need to decide how much of each section to cover in any given day. Select Learning Activities and Art Projects that fit your children's abilities and interests. Feel free to be creative and have fun as you lead your children into a real relationship with the Lord Jesus.

PRAYER AND MINISTRY TIME

Remember to choose a person who will receive prayer and ministry for this lesson. Help the children record this person's name in their Workbook. You should each agree to ask God to tell you something that will encourage that person. Refer to the prayer and ministry section of the Introduction, as needed.

Obeying God Is Best

TEACHING CONTENT

1. *Say*: Last week we learned about King Jehoshaphat.

   Ask: What kind of king was he?
   Did he love God?
   Did he listen to the Lord in his spirit?
   How did he handle his problem?
   [He asked God what he should do, and then he obeyed God.]

   Say: Sometimes when we have a problem, we forget to ask God for help or we decide to handle it ourselves. That is how the king in this lesson acted.

2. *Help the children find and read aloud* **1 Samuel 15:1.**
   "Samuel said to Saul, 'The Lord sent me to anoint you as king over his people Israel. So listen now to a message from him.'"

   Say: Saul was the king of Israel at this time. Samuel was a prophet of God who loved the Lord and helped the people worship and obey Him. God had Samuel begin by telling Saul to "listen."

3. *Find and read aloud* **1 Samuel 15:2-3.**
   The Lord who rules over all says, "I will punish the Amalekites because of what they did to Israel. As the Israelites came up from Egypt, the Amalekites attacked them. Now go. Attack the Amalekites. Completely destroy all that belongs to them. Do not spare the Amalekites. Put the men and women to death. Put the children and babies to death. Also kill the cattle, sheep, camels and donkeys."

   Say: God told Saul to destroy ALL of the Amalekites. This nation had tried to hurt God's people.

4. *Find and read aloud* **1 Samuel 15:7-9.**
   Saul attacked the Amalekites. He struck them down all the way from Havilah to Shur. Shur was near the eastern border of Egypt. Saul captured Agag, the king of the Amalekites. But he and his men totally destroyed with their swords all Agag's people. So Saul and the army spared Agag. They spared the best of the sheep and cattle. They spared the fat calves and lambs. They spared everything that was valuable. They weren't willing to completely destroy any of those things. But they totally destroyed everything that was worthless and weak.

   Say: The Lord was perfectly clear about what He wanted Saul to do. However, when Saul's army attacked the Amalekites, he saved their king, Agag, and some of the animals.

   Ask: Did Saul obey God?
   [No! Partly obeying is the same as disobeying.]

   Ask: How do you think Saul's disobedience made God feel?

5. *Find and read aloud* **1 Samuel 15:10-11.**
   "Then the Lord gave Samuel a message. He said, 'I am very sad I have made Saul king. He has turned away from me. He has not done what I directed him to do.' When Samuel heard that, he was

angry. He cried out to the Lord during that whole night."

Say: God was sorry that He had chosen Saul to be king over His people.

6. *Find and read aloud* **1 Samuel 15:13.**
"When Samuel got there, Saul said, 'May the Lord bless you. I've done what he directed me to do.'"

Ask: Was Saul telling the truth?
[No! Now Saul lied, saying that he had obeyed.]

Say: Samuel knew the truth because God had spoken to him.

7. *Find and read aloud* **1 Samuel 15:14-15.**
But Samuel said, "Then why do I hear the baaing of sheep? Why do I hear the mooing ofcattle?"
Saul answered, "The soldiers brought them from the Amalekites. They spared the best of the sheep and cattle. They did it to sacrifice them to the Lord your God. But we totally destroyed everything else."

Say: Saul did not want to admit he was wrong. He blamed his soldiers. Notice that Saul called the Lord "your God" and not "our God." This shows that he had turned away from God.

8. *Find and read aloud* **1 Samuel 15:16-19.**
"That's enough!" Samuel said to Saul. "Let me tell you what the Lord said to me last night."
"Tell me," Saul replied.
Samuel said, "There was a time when you didn't think you were important. But you became the leader of the tribes of Israel. The Lord anointed you to be king over Israel. He sent you to do something for him. He said, 'Go and completely destroy the Amalekites. Go and destroy those evil people. Fight against them until you have wiped them out.' Why didn't you obey the Lord? Why did you keep for yourselves what you had taken from your enemies? Why did you do what is evil in the sight of the Lord?"

Say: Samuel was able to hear God's voice clearly. He was obedient to tell King Saul what God had said.

9. *Find and read aloud* **1 Samuel 15:20-21.**
"But I did obey the Lord," Saul said. "I went to do what he sent me to do. I completely destroyed the Amalekites. I brought back Agag, their king. The soldiers took sheep and cattle from what had been taken from our enemies. They took the best of what had been set apart to God. They wanted to sacrifice them to the Lord your God at Gilgal."

Say: Again, Saul is lying. He did not feel sorry because he disobeyed God. He thought that if he sacrificed some of the animals, God would not be upset with him.

Ask: Have you ever been caught lying?
Do you think God knew you were lying?
[We can't hide anything from God.]

Say: Saul disobeyed and then tried to blame others for his disobedience.

Ask: Have you ever found yourself doing the same thing?

10. *Find and read aloud* **1 John 1:9.**
"…If we admit that we have sinned, he will forgive us our sins. He will forgive every wrong thing we have done. He will make us pure."

Say: When we disobey God, we need to admit that we have disobeyed and ask God for His forgiveness. When we are truly sorry, He promises to forgive us.

11. *Find and read aloud* **1 Samuel 15:22-23.**
But Samuel replied,
"What pleases the Lord more?
    Burnt offerings and sacrifices, or obeying the Lord?
It is better to obey than to offer a sacrifice.
    It is better to do what he says than to offer the fat of rams.

Refusing to obey the Lord is as sinful as using evil magic.
    Being proud is as evil as worshiping statues of gods.
You have refused to do what the Lord told you to do.
    So he has refused to have you as king."

Say: God said obeying Him is better than sacrificing to do some good deed He didn´t ask you to do.

12. *Find and read aloud* **1 Samuel 15:24.**
"Then Saul said to Samuel, 'I have sinned. I've broken the Lord's command. I haven't done what you directed me to do. I was afraid of the men. So I did what they said I should do.'"

Say: Now we find out what kept Saul from hearing and obeying God's voice. He was afraid of what other people would think. He was being led by his soul—his mind, will and emotions—instead of being led by the Holy Spirit.

Ask: Have you ever disobeyed because you were afraid of what other people would think?

Say: **WE NEED TO CARE MORE ABOUT WHAT GOD THINKS THAN ABOUT WHAT PEOPLE THINK**! We can't let other people keep us from hearing and obeying God's voice.

13. *Say*: We know that Saul did not hear and obey what God said because he was afraid of what his soldiers would say. Some reasons **WE** don't hear God's voice clearly are listed below:

a. We don't know **HOW** to hear God.
b. We don't spend time with God by reading the Bible, talking to Him or worshiping.
c. We have not confessed sins to God and received His forgiveness.
d. We have not forgiven someone.
e. We don't believe God is able to speak to us or help us.
f. We are afraid of what might happen if we obey God.
g. We are afraid of what people might think about us if we obey God.

Say: Turn to Lesson 8 in your Workbook. Let's look at Activity #3 together now. Which reasons on the list keep **YOU** from hearing God's voice clearly? Circle the reasons that are a problem in your life. Take some time now to pray to God, asking for His forgiveness. Ask Him to help you change in those areas.

LA #1, LA #2, LA #3, LA #4, LA #5, LA #6, AP #1

PRAYER AND MINISTRY TIME:

Take turns sharing what the Lord has given you to share with the person receiving ministry. Allow time now to hear anything more that the Lord wants to say.

Review the Prayer and Ministry Time section of the Introduction, as needed.

LEARNING ACTIVITIES

Activity #1 What keeps you from hearing and obeying God?

Have the children look at the list of things below that keep us from hearing God clearly. Have them circle the things that are a problem in their life.

a. We don't know how to hear God.

b. We don't spend time with God by reading the Bible, talking to Him or worshiping.

c. We have not confessed sins to God and received His forgiveness.

d. We have not forgiven someone.

e. We don't believe God is able to speak to us or help us.

f. We are afraid of what might happen if we obey God.

g. We are afraid of what people might think about us if we obey God.

Encourage them to write a prayer to God, asking for His forgiveness and help in those areas.

Activity #2 Which king is it?

Have the children write on the lines below the names of the kings that match the lists underneath. Which words describe King Saul? Which words describe King Jehoshaphat?

_____   _____

Knew God well

Depended on God's help

Wanted to please God

When wrong, was truly sorry

Knew and loved God´s Word

Never turned away from God

Didn't know God well

Depended on himself and others

Wanted to please others

When wrong, made excuses or lied

Didn't know or love what God said in scripture or through his prophet

Turned away from God

Activity #3 Watch a video about God rejecting Saul as king.

MATERIALS NEEDED: A phone or computer with internet access

Search YouTube for a video titled "Samuel Rebukes King Saul – Superbook" and watch it together. Ask the children what they think of this video.

Activity #4 Jesus washes us whiter than snow.

MATERIALS NEEDED: Plastic knives, ingredients for chocolate cupcakes and liners, or chocolate graham crackers, ingredients for white frosting.

Help the children bake chocolate cupcakes and frost them with white frosting. The dark cupcake represents our sin and the white frosting represents us when we have been cleansed whiter than snow by Jesus. If you choose to, you could use chocolate graham crackers instead of baking cupcakes, or spread cream cheese on dark bread.

Activity #5 Play Chutes and Ladders.

MATERIALS NEEDED: The board game Chutes and Ladders

Together, play the board game Chutes and Ladders. The game shows how one move can make you go in a completely different direction. Have the children answer the question: Can you think of a decision that you made that changed the direction in your life? Have the children write about it in their workbook.

Activity #6 Watch a video about making choices and obeying God.

MATERIALS NEEDED: A phone or computer with internet access

Search YouTube for the video "Do the Bright Thing" 1/3 and 2/3 from the McGee and Me series by Focus on the Family.

Have the children write in their Workbook the answers to these questions:
Did the main character seem more like King Jehoshaphat or King Saul? Why do you think that?

ART PROJECT

Project #1 Jesus is King.

MATERIALS NEEDED: Lesson 8 crown pattern, gold construction paper, crayons, scissors, "jewel" stickers, stapler or tape

Have the children create a crown to wear. Using the Lesson 8 crown pattern found in the Workbook, trace sections of a crown on gold-colored paper. Cut out enough crown sections so that stapled or taped together, they fit on your child's head. Before attaching the ends, write "Jesus is King" on the crown and decorate it. When the children are finished, attach the ends of the crown together so it will fit on their head.

Say: Jesus is King of our lives when we listen to the Holy Spirit in our spirit. We make ourselves king, instead of Jesus, when we listen to our soul and do something that God would not want us to do.

Ask: Who will rule in your life?

LESSON 9

HEARING GOD THROUGH THE INNER KNOWING

OBJECTIVE

God often communicates through an inner knowing. When God speaks to us through an inner knowing, He does not use words. Instead, He gives us either a "knowing that you know," a sense of peace, a sudden lack of peace, or the idea to slow down and wait.

HEARING GOD THROUGH THE INNER KNOWING

LESSON 9 CONTENT OBJECTIVE

To understand that God often communicates through an inner knowing. When God speaks to us through an inner knowing, He does not use words. Instead, He gives us either a "knowing that you know," a sense of peace, a sudden lack of peace, or the idea to slow down and wait.

LESSON 9 KEY SCRIPTURE

Each day read aloud this lesson's scripture. Have the children write it out in the Workbook in the space provided. Encourage them to memorize this lesson's verse by the end of the week. Challenge the children to recite it without reading it.

Isaiah 41:13 "I am the LORD your God. I take hold of your right hand. I say to you, 'Do not be afraid. I will help you.'"

LESSON 9 READING ASSIGNMENT

Read Chapters 13 and 14 in *Is That Really You, God?*
Some children will need you to read portions of the assigned reading to them, others can read the chapters on their own or take turns reading aloud as a group.

TEACHING CONTENT, LEARNING ACTIVITIES AND ART PROJECTS

These are the largest components of the lesson. Depending upon your children's ages, you will need to decide how much of each section to cover in any given day. Select Learning Activities and Art Projects that fit your children's abilities and interests. Feel free to be creative and have fun as you lead your children into a real relationship with the Lord Jesus.

PRAYER AND MINISTRY TIME

Remember to choose a person who will receive prayer and ministry for this lesson. Help the children record this person's name in their Workbook. You should each agree to ask God to tell you something that will encourage that person. Refer to the prayer and ministry section of the Introduction, as needed.

Hearing God Through the Inner Knowing

TEACHING CONTENT

1. *Ask:* Have you ever been shown the way to a new place?

   Say: God can use the inner knowing to guide us in new situations. Imagine that you are walking down the street with your mother, hand in hand, not saying a word. You come to a crosswalk, and the signal says "Don't Walk."

   Ask: What do you do?
   [Hopefully, you stop!]

   Say: When the signal says "Walk," you cross the street together. Your mother does not need to say anything to you, as she holds your hand and leads you. Next, you come to a crosswalk where there is no signal. But there is a policeman, who guides the traffic. He holds up his hand in your direction, so you stop. Finally, he waves you on. Now you know you can walk across the street. You knew what to do, even though the policeman did not speak to you. You watched him, and you were still holding your mother's hand, and you followed what she showed you to do.

2. *Say:* Often, the Holy Spirit guides or leads us without using words. We call that an "inner knowing." Instead of speaking words, God may give us a sense that we KNOW that we know, a sense of peace, a sudden lack of peace, or the idea to slow down and wait.

   a. **A "KNOWING THAT YOU KNOW"**
   Some people with an inner knowing say that they have an intuition or a holy hunch. They just KNOW what God wants them to do.

   For example, a new child moves onto your block. You, who are normally very shy, just "know that you know" that God wants you to invite the new neighbor to come over and play. The idea may just come into your mind, "I am supposed to ask that new kid to play."

   b. **A FEELING OF PEACE THAT SHOWS YOU HAVE GOD′S "GREEN LIGHT"**
   When God wants you to do something, He will give you a "green light" or go ahead signal. Your mind might come up with reasons not to do it, but the more you pray about it, the better you feel about it inside.[1]

   You might see something that needs to be done and you sense a green light from God to meet that need. For example, you are on your driveway playing and you see that litter has blown into your yard. You see it and sense God saying to pick it up. You stop playing for a minute and throw it in the trash.

   Or your sister's jacket has fallen off the hook onto the floor. You see it, and you sense a green light from God to hang it back up.

   Or you are playing with a friend and the thought comes to mind to invite him to go to church with you. You are afraid that your friend will say no, but the more you pray about it, the more you think you should ask him now.

c. **AN UNEASINESS OR LACK OF PEACE THAT CAUSES YOU TO STOP AND THINK**

If God doesn't want you to do something, He will speak to you through your spirit with a "red light," or a lack of peace.[2] Your mind may tell you to go ahead and do it. However, if you listen to that inner knowing, you will stay in God's will.

For example, you are playing with a friend at your home and your mother has told you that the cookies on the counter are not to be eaten until after dinner. Your friend tells you that you should sneak a cookie anyway. You feel uneasy about the idea of sneaking a cookie. This uneasiness is a red light from the Holy Spirit.

Or you are riding your bike to a friend's house and a stranger wants you to stop to talk. You suddenly feel uneasy about this person. This uneasiness is a red light signal from the Holy Spirit, telling you to **NOT** talk to this person and to ride away quickly.

d. **AN IDEA TO SLOW DOWN AND WAIT**

This is like getting a yellow light. God may be saying that you are not to do something just **NOW**. You should wait because the timing is not right. For example, you want your father to drive you to the store to buy something you need. You come into the room where your father is, but you sense that now is not the right time to ask. This is a yellow light from the Holy Spirit, signaling you to wait until later.

3. *Say*: We often want God to tell us what He wants us to do. It is just as important to know what God does **NOT** want us to do and where he does **NOT** want us to go.

   Ask: Have you ever been in a place where you knew God didn't want you to be?
       What did you feel like inside?
   [That is the inner knowing and God was giving you a red light.]

   Say: The inner knowing is just as supernatural as hearing from God through visions or dreams. An inner knowing is just not as exciting or spectacular.[3] Sometimes you may need to wait on the Lord to have that inner knowing. If you don't know what to do, then you need to take time alone to pray and wait on God.[4] Don't be pushed into deciding what to do when you don't have a clear inner knowing from God.

LA #1

4. *Say*: When the Holy Spirit guides us, what He is asking us to do may seem difficult. Sometimes we are not comfortable with going to new places or doing new things. Our lesson today tells about Peter when he did something new for the very first time.

5. *Help the children find and read aloud* **Matthew 14:22-24.**
   Right away Jesus made the disciples get into the boat. He had them go on ahead of him to the other side of the Sea of Galilee. Then he sent the crowd away. After he had sent them away, he went up on a mountainside by himself to pray. Later that night, he was there alone. The boat was already a long way from land. It was being pounded by the waves because the wind was blowing against it.

   Say: Jesus wanted to be alone and pray to His Father, God, so He sent the disciples on ahead of Him. But during the night when the disciples were in the boat, a wind began to blow and toss the boat. Sailing a boat that is being tossed by a strong wind is hard work, but some of the disciples were fishermen and were used to doing this.

6. *Find and read aloud* **Matthew 14:25-27.**

> **"Shortly before dawn, Jesus went out to the disciples. He walked on the lake. They saw him walking on the lake and were terrified. 'It's a ghost!' they said. And they cried out in fear.**
> **Right away Jesus called out to them, 'Be brave! It is I. Don't be afraid.'"**

Say: Jesus walked across the water to them in the boat, perhaps to help them. The disciples did not know it was Jesus. It frightened them to see someone walking on the water.

Ask: Can you imagine seeing someone walking on top of the water like that?
How would you feel if you saw that?

7. *Find and read aloud* **Matthew 14:28-29.**

> **"'Lord, is it you?' Peter asked. 'If it is, tell me to come to you on the water.' 'Come,' Jesus said. So Peter got out of the boat. He walked on the water toward Jesus."**

Say: Sometimes Peter was impulsive—he did not always stop to think about what he was doing. In this case, it was good because he just obeyed. He had an inner knowing that was like a green light. He just KNEW he would be able to walk on the water if Jesus told him to come to Him. And he DID walk on the water—for a while.

8. *Find and read aloud* **Matthew 14:30-32.**

> **But when Peter saw the wind, he was afraid. He began to sink. He cried out, "Lord! Save me!"**
> **Right away Jesus reached out his hand and caught him. "Your faith is so small!" he said. "Why did you doubt me?"**
> **When they climbed into the boat, the wind died down.**

Say: Peter listened to the inner knowing at first. Then, he started to look at the things around him instead of looking only at Jesus. He thought, "How can I walk on water?" This seemed too hard. When Peter began to sink, Jesus reached out His hand to help him and to guide him back to the boat. Too bad Peter didn't just remember what God was saying to him through that inner knowing! He could have walked on water longer.

Sometimes the Holy Spirit will ask us to do new things. We may feel like Peter did when he stepped out of the boat onto the water. It may seem hard or even impossible at times. However, if we keep looking to Jesus and remember what the Holy Spirit has said, He will guide us to where we need to go.

LA #2

9. *Find and read aloud* **Acts 16:6-10.**

> **Paul and his companions traveled all through the area of Phrygia and Galatia. The Holy Spirit had kept them from preaching the word in Asia Minor. They came to the border of Mysia. From there they tried to enter Bithynia. But the Spirit of Jesus would not let them. So they passed by Mysia. Then they went down to Troas. During the night Paul had a vision. He saw a man from Macedonia standing and begging him. "Come over to Macedonia!" the man said. "Help us!" After Paul had seen the vision, we got ready at once to leave for Macedonia. We decided that God had called us to preach the good news there.**

Say: This is another Bible passage with an example of God guiding through the inner knowing. Paul and his friends thought they would go tell people about Jesus in Asia Minor and Bithynia. However, the Holy Spirit would not let them. The Holy Spirit used the inner knowing to tell them not to go there.

Ask: What do you think that was like?

[It could have come in the form of a sudden uneasiness: a red light in their spirits.]

Say: So they obeyed God and went to Troas instead. Then, God showed Paul where He wanted them to go by giving him a vision. It turns out that God had prepared the heart of a woman from Macedonia named Lydia to ask Jesus into her life (**Acts 16:14**).

10. *Find and read aloud* **Acts 20:22-24.**

> **Now I am going to Jerusalem. The Holy Spirit compels me. I don't know what will happen to me there. I only know that in every city the Spirit warns me. He tells me that I will face prison and suffering. But my life means nothing to me. My only goal is to finish the race. I want to complete the work the Lord Jesus has given me. He wants me to tell others about the good news of God's grace.**

Say: Before, in **Acts 16:6-10**, God was giving a red light. In this passage, God gave Paul a green light. God needed Paul to preach in Jerusalem. Paul said that he was COMPELLED to go, which means God convinced him to go. Paul really wanted to preach to the rulers in Jerusalem, who did not know Jesus. The Holy Spirit gave him an inner knowing about the danger—Paul just KNEW THAT HE KNEW that he would go to prison there.

What is amazing is that Paul WANTED to go to Jerusalem to finish the job God had given him! God is so good; He gets our hearts ready to be able to obey Him.

Ask: Who else do you know from the Bible who went to Jerusalem to finish the job God the Father gave him?

[Jesus also went to Jerusalem to finish what He was called to do (**Luke 9:51**).]

11. *Find and read aloud* **John 10:27-28.**

> **"My sheep listen to my voice. I know them, and they follow me. I give them eternal life, and they will never die. No one will steal them out of my hand."**

Say: This verse talks about being held by Jesus' hand. As we obey the inner knowing, we can go through life as if our hand is in Jesus' hand.

LA #3, AP #1, AP #2

PRAYER AND MINISTRY TIME

Take turns sharing what the Lord has given you to share with the person receiving ministry. Allow time now to hear anything more that the Lord wants to say.

Review the Prayer and Ministry Time section of the Introduction, as needed.

LEARNING ACTIVITIES

Activity #1 Play the game Follow Your Guide.
MATERIALS NEEDED: A blindfold

To play, place a blindfold on a child. Assure him that you will guide him across a room with obstacles, so that he is not hurt. You will guide him without saying a word. Take his hand and silently walk across the room together, intermittently walking and stopping, moving around items in the way. Then trade roles by placing the blindfold on yourself and letting the child be the guide.

You could also place the children in pairs—one a guide and the other blindfolded. The guide should lead the other child around the room without using words, but guiding them to go or stop, as you showed them. Then, have them switch roles.

Have them answer the following questions in the Workbook:
What it was like to be guided without words? Did you understand what your guide was trying to say to you? How difficult was it to follow his directions when he couldn't use words? Write about what it was like to be blindfolded and led.

Activity #2 Play Red Light/Green Light.
This game is played as follows:
- One person plays the role of "traffic light" and the rest try to touch him. To start, all the children form a line more than 30 feet away from the traffic light.
- The traffic light faces away from the line of kids and calls "Green light." Then the kids are allowed to move towards the traffic light, to try to touch him.
- At any point, the traffic light may call "Red light!" and then turn around. All of the children who are caught moving after he turns around are "out" and must sit down.
- Play resumes when the traffic light turns back around and calls "Green light."
- The traffic light wins if all the children are out before anyone is able to touch him. Otherwise, the first player to touch the traffic light wins the game and earns the right to be the traffic light for the next game.

Activity #3 Act out the scriptures with a resistance band.
MATERIALS NEEDED: A stretchy resistance band

First, use the stretchy band to be like the Holy Spirit in **Acts 16:6-10**. In these verses the Holy Spirit kept Paul from going into Asia Minor and Bithynia. Obviously, the Holy Spirit does not use stretchy bands! Have the children write how the Holy Spirit may have told Paul not to go there.

Then, use the stretchy band to be like the Holy Spirit in **Acts 20:22-24**. In these verses, the Holy Spirit compelled Paul to want to go to Jerusalem. Again, the Holy Spirit does not use stretchy bands! Write below how Paul might have known that the Holy Spirit wanted him to go to Jerusalem.

ART PROJECTS

Project #1 Make a traffic light.
If the children have already made a traffic light, look at one together now. If they did not complete the traffic light art project listed in Lesson 4, make it now.

MATERIALS NEEDED:
For the easy version—Red and green construction paper, a popsicle stick and glue
For the more difficult version—Red, green and white construction paper, a paint stirring stick, crayons, and glue

Have the children make a traffic light.

Say: We obey God for our own safety, just as we have to obey traffic lights and road signs for our safety.

a. Easy version – Using the Lesson 4 circle pattern in the Workbook, trace and cut out one red and one green circle (the same size) out of construction paper and glue them on opposite sides of a Popsicle stick.

b. More difficult version – Cut a piece of white construction paper in half lengthwise (so that you have two tall and skinny pieces.) Glue these together with the paint stirring stick between them. Leave some stick exposed at the bottom so you can hold it up. Using the Lesson 4 circle pattern in the Workbook, trace three 3-inch circles on both sides in a line up and down. Use a crayon to color the red and yellow circles on one side, and the green and yellow circles on the other side. The correct order of the colors is red at the top, yellow in the middle, and green at the bottom. Using the circle pattern, trace and cut out one red circle from construction paper for one side and one green circle for the other side, and glue them on. These will seem brighter and easier to see than the other "lights" on the traffic light.

Using the traffic light visual aid, explain the following:
The Holy Spirit sometimes tells us, in our spirit, to stop, like a red light. This feels like a sudden lack of peace, and you feel uneasy inside. Sometimes the Holy Spirit tells us to wait, like the yellow light. Other times He will say "Go," like the green light, and we feel peaceful or excited inside. We must be sure to listen to the Lord, so we can obey Him. Sometimes it takes a while before we know what God wants us to do.

The Lord may lead us to do new things, but He will be with us to help us. For example, He may want you to be a friend to a new boy or girl at church, and give you a green light to be friendly. Or the Holy Spirit may tell you to stop watching a TV program that might scare you, giving you a red light. The Lord may have you be quiet and listen when you are upset, giving you a yellow light, to wait before you act.

Think of situations in which the Lord could speak to you using a green, yellow or red light.

Project #2 Color in the traffic light.
MATERIALS NEEDED: Red, yellow and green markers or crayons

Have the children color in the Traffic Light coloring page in the back of the Workbook. Ask them to describe how a traffic light can be like hearing the inner knowing.

LESSON 10

HEARING GOD THROUGH THE SOFT, INNER VOICE

OBJECTIVE

Sometimes God speaks to us through the inner voice. This is when the Holy Spirit speaks in a quiet voice using words. We need to listen carefully to hear God's soft voice.

HEARING GOD THROUGH THE SOFT, INNER VOICE

LESSON 10 CONTENT OBJECTIVE

To understand that sometimes God speaks to us through the inner voice. This is when the Holy Spirit speaks in a quiet voice using words. We need to listen carefully to hear God's soft voice.

LESSON 10 KEY SCRIPTURE

Each day read aloud this lesson's scripture. Have the children write it out in the Workbook in the space provided. Encourage them to memorize this lesson's verse by the end of the week. Challenge the children to recite it without reading it.

Isaiah 30:21 "You will hear your Teacher's voice behind you. You will hear it whether you turn to the right or the left. It will say, 'Here is the path I want you to take. So walk on it.'"

LESSON 10 READING ASSIGNMENT

Read Chapter 15 in *Is That Really You, God?*
Some children will need you to read portions of the assigned reading to them, others can read the chapters on their own or take turns reading aloud as a group.

TEACHING CONTENT, LEARNING ACTIVITIES AND ART PROJECTS

These are the largest components of the lesson. Depending upon your children's ages, you will need to decide how much of each section to cover in any given day. Select Learning Activities and Art Projects that fit your children's abilities and interests. Feel free to be creative and have fun as you lead your children into a real relationship with the Lord Jesus.

PRAYER AND MINISTRY TIME

Remember to choose a person who will receive prayer and ministry for this lesson. Help the children record this person's name in their Workbook. You should each agree to ask God to tell you something that will encourage that person. Refer to the prayer and ministry section of the Introduction, as needed.

Hearing God Through the Soft, Inner Voice

TEACHING CONTENT

1. *Say:* In the last lesson we talked about the **INNER KNOWING.**

   Ask: What is that like?

   [It is as if God is leading you by the hand. He does **NOT** use words. Instead, He gives you a "knowing that you know" inside you. Or sometimes the inner knowing is like a traffic signal—a sense of peace like a green light telling you to go, a sudden lack of peace like a red light telling you to stop, or a yellow light telling you to slow down and wait.]

2. *Say:* The Holy Spirit can also use words to speak to us. We do not hear that voice with our ears (*point to your ear*).

   Ask: What part of us hears the voice of the Holy Spirit?
   Is it our spirit, soul or body?
   [We hear God in our spirit where the Holy Spirit lives inside of us (*point to your upper abdomen*). It's like having ears in our spirit.]

   Say: God may speak loudly or softly.

   Ask: How do you sound when you speak in a loud voice? (*Say something loudly.*)
   How do you sound when you speak in a soft voice? (*Say something in a soft voice.*)

   Say: When the Holy Spirit uses a soft voice we call that the **INNER VOICE.** It is a soft voice using words we understand. Sometimes we need to listen carefully to hear God's soft voice.

3. *Help the children find and read aloud* **Isaiah 30:21.**
   "You will hear your Teacher's voice behind you. You will hear it whether you turn to the right or the left. It will say, 'Here is the path I want you to take. So walk on it.'"

   Say: God has placed the Holy Spirit in our spirit to be our Teacher, who will guide us. When the Holy Spirit uses the inner voice, He can be so soft that it is easy to ignore what He says. Ignoring the inner voice of God can be a **BIG** mistake. It was a big mistake for a young man named Craig, who was on a church softball team. Here is his true story:

   > We were in a softball tournament and that night we had a game. During the day the Lord spoke softly to me—that I would get hit by the ball. Well, I didn't pay attention to it; I just forgot about it. I usually played outfield, but that evening they asked me to play shortstop. A player on the other team came up to bat and when he hit the ball, it took a funny bounce right in front of me. The way it bounced made it hard to catch and it hit me smack in the face. It knocked me out! When I came to, everyone was standing over me, praying for me.

   > Some friends brought me home and told my folks that I had been hit in the head pretty hard. My eye was swollen, bruised, and already bloodshot. My mom wasn't sure what to put on it because it was so tender to the touch. After my friends left, my mom said to me, "Craig, you must really hurt."

I said, "Yes, I do, but it is not from the pain of my eye. I hurt because God spoke to me and told me that I would get hit today, and I ignored His voice. When will I learn?" I felt worse about not listening to God than I did about my black eye. God's voice was so small. It was easy to ignore.

Many people have asked me since then, "What should you do if God says something like that to you?" I tell them, "Ask God what to do. Ask Him for protection. Ask Him for direction." There is no reason God would have said that to me unless He wanted to tell me how to protect myself. God cares very much about our bodies and He wants to speak to us, His children.

Ask: Can you tell about a time when you heard God speaking to you with words in a soft voice?

LA #1, LA #2, AP #1

4. *Find and read aloud* **Mark 2:1-4.**
   A few days later, Jesus entered Capernaum again. The people heard that he had come home. So many people gathered that there was no room left. There was not even room outside the door. And Jesus preached the word to them. Four of those who came were carrying a man who could not walk. But they could not get him close to Jesus because of the crowd. So they made a hole by digging through the roof above Jesus. Then they lowered the man through it on a mat.

Say: This man was paralyzed—he could not walk. Thankfully, he had four good friends who wanted to take him to Jesus. They believed Jesus could heal him. But, when they got to the house, it was full of people. There was no room to go through the door, so they dug through the roof to get him to Jesus! That really showed their faith in Jesus' healing power.

5. *Find and read aloud* **Mark 2:5-7.**
   "Jesus saw their faith. So he said to the man, 'Son, your sins are forgiven.' Some teachers of the law were sitting there. They were thinking, 'Why is this fellow talking like that? He's saying a very evil thing! Only God can forgive sins!'"

Say: This is a Bible passage in which Jesus heard the Holy Spirit talk to Him. The people who were in the house heard what Jesus said. Some of them began thinking in their hearts that Jesus was wrong. How could Jesus forgive sins? They thought, "Only God can forgive sins." They did not believe Jesus was God's Son.

Now, Jesus could not hear their thoughts, but He COULD hear the Holy Spirit telling him what they were thinking. We do not have the exact words that the Holy Spirit used, but we know what Jesus said.

6. *Find and read aloud* **Mark 2:8-9.**
   "Right away Jesus knew what they were thinking. So he said to them, 'Why are you thinking these things? Is it easier to say to this man, "Your sins are forgiven"? Or to say, "Get up, take your mat and walk"?'"

Ask: Which do you think is harder?
   Is it harder to just say the words, "Your sins are forgiven" or to actually heal someone who can't walk?
   [It is harder to heal a man who can't walk. The teachers of the law must have thought the same thing.]

7. *Find and read aloud* **Mark 2:10-12.**
   "But I want you to know that the Son of Man has authority on earth to forgive sins." So

Jesus spoke to the man who could not walk. "I tell you," he said, "get up. Take your mat and go home." The man got up and took his mat. Then he walked away while everyone watched. All the people were amazed. They praised God and said, "We have never seen anything like this!"

Say: Sometimes Jesus called Himself by the name "the Son of Man." He was saying that He DID have the right and the power to forgive sins. And He proved it by healing the man who was paralyzed. Jesus could do both—forgive sins and heal people.

Ask: So, how did Jesus know what the people in the house were thinking?
    [The Holy Spirit told Him.]

Ask: Did the Holy Spirit speak so that everyone in the room could hear?
    [No, but Jesus knew what the Holy Spirit spoke in His spirit.]

Say: The Holy Spirit can speak to US in our spirit too. He often speaks in a soft voice. We must be still to hear the Holy Spirit inside of us.

8. *Say*: When we pray and are talking to God, we can ask Him a question. He may answer right away or He may wait to answer. We need to be quiet and listen for His answer.

    • Sometimes we hear inside us a soft voice giving us a message with words.

    • Sometimes the Holy Spirit will bring a specific Bible verse to mind. We will suddenly think of that verse. This is why it is important to memorize scriptures—so that God can use them to speak to us.

    • Sometimes God will tell us where we can find a verse. For example, we might hear Him say, **"John 10:27."** Then, when we look up that verse we will know what God is saying to us.

    • We may find our answer as we read God's Word every day. The Bible is like God's letter to us. When we read the Bible, sometimes the Holy Spirit makes a specific verse seem important to us. That verse catches our attention so we know that God is saying those words to us.

9. When we hear God speak in a soft voice in our spirit, no one else can hear the words that we hear. They will be soft and inside of us. God knows what we are thinking. He cares about us and helps us.

    LA #3, LA #4, AP #2

PRAYER AND MINISTRY TIME:

Take turns sharing what the Lord has given you to say to the person receiving ministry. Allow time now to hear anything more that the Lord wants to say.

Review the Prayer and Ministry Time section of the Introduction, as needed.

LEARNING ACTIVITIES

Activity #1 Play the game "Hot or Cold."
MATERIALS NEEDED: A child or an object to hide

Before you begin this game, hide something that the children must find. Then when you are ready to play the game, tell one child that you will give him help to find a hidden object by giving directions in a soft voice. Speak softly in order to sound like the Holy Spirit speaking in his spirit with the inner voice. Whisper "warm" when the child is going in the right direction toward the hidden object, "cold" when he is going in the wrong direction, and "hot" when he is very close to the hidden object. You can play this repeatedly until each child learns to follow that still, small voice. After playing the game, have the children write in their Workbook about what it was like to hear and follow the whispered guidance. Alternatively, instead of looking for a hidden object, your child can look for a hidden sibling or friend.

Have the children write in the Workbook about trying to follow the directions in the soft, whispered voice. They are asked: Did it take a while to figure out which direction to go? How hard was it to hear the whispered words?

Activity #2 Play the Quiet Sound Bingo game.
MATERIALS NEEDED: A Sound Bingo game or a home-made Quiet Sound Bingo game, which requires the following:
> Two 8 ½ x 11-inch pieces of card stock, scissors, ruler, pencil, colored markers, copies of the Lesson 10 sound pictures, glue, six tokens/child (pennies, poker chips, dried pasta or Cheerios), 12 index cards, pen or pencil, a bottle of water, glass, pencil with an eraser and paper, a piece of paper to rip, hard cover book, two dice, pen that clicks, scotch tape dispenser, pepper grinder, cracker

You may either order a Sound Bingo game online or create your own game. Directions to make a game can be found below in this lesson's "Art Projects" section. An example of a ready-made game you could order online is Soundtracks sold at Montessoriservices.com. It is designed to sharpen listening and concentration skills of children 4 years and up. It includes a CD, bingo game boards and markers. If you purchase a ready-made game, follow the directions that come with it. If you make your own, follow the directions below.

Preparing to play—
Say: When God speaks to us in a quiet voice, we need to be still to hear what God is saying. This game will help us practice careful listening and recognizing what we hear.

Distribute the game boards, one per player. Give each player six tokens. Erect a visual barrier between you and the children so that they cannot see what you are using to make each sound.

To play—The sounds should be made randomly. To do this, shuffle the index cards and place the pile face down. Make the sound on each card as you turn it over. Allow about 10 seconds of silence between sounds. The children should place a token on the square with the picture that matches the sound they hear. Each game board will have only six sound-pictures, so every player will not be able to match every sound you make. However, if you are using all the game boards, someone will mark a sound picture each time. Whoever is first to place a token on every picture on his game board should call out, "BINGO!" Check that child's game board against the pile of cards that you have already turned over. If the child is correct, announce a winner and award a prize.

After playing the game, have the children write in their Workbook about what it was like to try to hear and recognize the sounds. They are asked: Was it easy or hard to recognize the soft sounds and match them to a picture? Did you have to wait a long time to hear a sound that matched a picture on your game board? Did you win a game?

Activity #3 Play the Scripture Hunt game.

MATERIALS NEEDED: Sticky notes, scissors, pen or pencil

Before the children play this game, write on a sticky note each of the scripture verses and directions listed. Write on the blank line the location of the next clue. The directions will say what action the children should take as they move to the next clue. The actions will be related to the scripture on that sticky note (see underlined words). Hide the clues appropriately. You might want to place the clues in plastic Easter eggs, and then hide the eggs.

Begin the game by giving the children Clue #1. Help them read the instructions:

Clue #1
Galatians 5:25 "If we live by the Spirit, let us also <u>walk</u> in the Spirit." <u>Walk</u> to _____*(e.g the bookshelf).* When the children get to that location, they should look for a sticky note with a scripture verse on it. When they find it, they should read that verse aloud and then go to the next clue's hiding place, using the action indicated.

Clue #2
Psalm 119:32 "I am <u>quick</u> to follow your commands, because you have added to my understanding." <u>Run</u> to _____*(e.g the television).*

Clue #3
Psalm 47:1 "<u>Clap</u> your hands, all you nations. Shout to God with cries of joy." <u>Clap</u> until you get to _____.

Clue #4
Ephesians 6:17 "Put on the helmet of salvation. And take the sword of the Holy Spirit. The <u>sword</u> is God's word." <u>Carry your Bible</u> to_____.

Clue #5
Psalm 63:4 "I will praise you as long as I live. I will call on your name when I <u>lift up</u> my hands in prayer." <u>Raise hands</u> as you go to _____.

Clue #6
John 16:13 "But when the Spirit of truth comes, he will <u>guide</u> you into all the truth. He will not speak on his own. He will speak only what he hears. And he will tell you what is still going to happen." <u>Guide a person near you by taking his hand</u> to _____.

Clue #7
Psalm 119:10 "I trust in you with all my heart. Don't let me <u>wander</u> away from your commands." <u>Wander</u> to the _____.

Clue #8
Micah 3:8a "The Spirit of the Lord has filled me with <u>power</u>. He helps me do what is fair. He makes me brave." <u>Flex your muscles</u> as you go to _____.

Clue #9
Matthew 11:28 "Come to me, all you who are tired and are carrying heavy loads. I will give you <u>rest</u>." <u>Sit down and rest!</u> The end.

Have the children look at the scriptures on clues #1 through #9. Have each of them decide which scripture seems the most important to them in their life right now. Have them write out that scripture in their Workbook and explain why it is important to them.

Activity #4 Make peanut butter and jelly sandwiches.

MATERIALS NEEDED: A plate, sliced bread, peanut butter, jelly, a knife

As the children make their own sandwich, say, "Just as the peanut butter and jelly work together inside the pieces of bread, the Holy Spirit and God's Word work together inside of us. The Holy Spirit can use Scripture to say something to help us. Both the Holy Spirit and the Bible remind us how much Jesus loves us."

Have the children write about how the Holy Spirit and God's Word work together inside us. In the Workbook they are asked: Has the Holy Spirit ever spoken to you through a verse? If so, which verse was it and what do you think He was saying to you?

ART PROJECTS:

Project #1 Create a Quiet Sound Bingo Game.

MATERIALS NEEDED:

For game boards: Two 8 ½ x 11-inch pieces of card stock, scissors, ruler, pencil, colored markers, copies of the Lesson 10 sound-pictures, glue

For game markers: pennies, poker chips, dried pasta or cheerios

For choosing the sounds: 12 index cards, pen or pencil

For sound-making: a bottle of water, glass, pencil with an eraser and paper, piece of paper to rip, hardcover book, two dice, pen that clicks, Scotch tape dispenser, pepper grinder, cracker.

To create your own Quiet Sound Bingo game, make four bingo game boards and 12 sound index cards. Gather six markers per player.

To make four game boards, cut in half two 8 ½ x 11-inch pieces of card stock. With a pencil and a ruler, draw a grid of lines, dividing each of the four game boards into six squares. In each square, glue a picture of an item that makes a quiet sound. Make enough copies of the sound-pictures to fill in the squares of four different game boards. The sound-pictures are listed in the parentheses below. From the 14 suggested sounds, select the 12 sounds you will make. Include a different mix of pictures on all four game boards. Make sure every sound that you will make is represented on at least one game board. Possible sounds could include items on the list below, or you may think of other sounds to make. Write your 12 sounds (found in bold) on index cards.

- **water** – slowly pour water into a glass (the drop of water)
- **eraser** – erase a pencil mark with a pencil eraser (the pencil with an eraser)
- **owl** – quietly say, "Hoo, Hoo" (the owl)
- **wind** – blow continuously through pursed lips (the cloud blowing wind)
- **ripping paper** – slowly rip a piece of paper (the rectangle with a jagged line halfway through it)
- **knock** – quietly knock on a book (the door)
- **bird** – if you can, make a bird sound by whistling (the bird)
- **dice** – roll the dice on the table (the two dice)
- **clicking pen** – click a pen open and shut (the pen that clicks)
- **scotch tape** – rip off a piece of tape from the dispenser (the scotch tape dispenser)
- **panting** – stick your tongue out and pant like a dog (the dog)

- **knuckles** – If you can, crack your knuckles (the hand)
- **pepper** – turn a pepper grinder a few times (the pepper grinder)
- **cracker** – crunch a cracker (the cracker)

Project #2 Make a Bible bookmark.

MATERIALS NEEDED: Card stock, ruler, scissors, a hole punch, ribbon or yarn, markers or crayons

Have the children make a bookmark that they can use to mark their place in a Bible. Have them cut out a piece of card stock about 6 inches long and 2 inches wide. Cut a piece of ribbon, or yarn, 8 inches long. Punch a hole ¼ inch from the top and insert one end of the ribbon through it. Tie a knot in the ribbons at the top of the bookmark, so that the two loose ends can be seen when the bookmark is in a Bible. Encourage the children to draw a picture or design on the bookmark. Or they could write out a favorite verse on it.

LESSON 11

HEARING GOD THROUGH THE LOUD VOICE OF THE HOLY SPIRIT

OBJECTIVE

*Sometimes God speaks to us in a loud voice using words.
It can also be called the authoritative voice of the Holy Spirit.
It seems so loud that we think people around us can hear
it too, but they can't. The Holy Spirit speaks these
loud words in our spirit.*

HEARING GOD THROUGH THE LOUD VOICE OF THE HOLY SPIRIT

LESSON 11 CONTENT OBJECTIVE

To understand that sometimes God speaks to us in a loud voice using words. It can also be called the authoritative voice of the Holy Spirit. It seems so loud that we think people around us can hear it too, but they can't. The Holy Spirit speaks these loud words in our spirit.

Each day read aloud this lesson's scripture. Have the children write it out in the Workbook in the space provided. Encourage them to memorize this lesson's verse by the end of the week. Challenge the children to recite it without reading it.

1 Samuel 3:10 "The Lord came and called as before. He said, 'Samuel! Samuel!' And Samuel replied, 'Speak, your servant is listening'" (NLT).

You may want to shorten the verse for younger children: **1 Samuel 3:10 "And Samuel replied, 'Speak, your servant is listening'" (NLT).**

LESSON 11 READING ASSIGNMENT

Read Chapter 16 in *Is That Really You, God?*
Some children will need you to read portions of the assigned reading to them, others can read the chapters on their own or take turns reading aloud as a group.

TEACHING CONTENT, LEARNING ACTIVITIES AND ART PROJECTS

These are the largest components of the lesson. Depending upon your children's ages, you will need to decide how much of each section to cover in any given day. Select Learning Activities and Art Projects that fit your children's abilities and interests. Feel free to be creative and have fun as you lead your children into a real relationship with the Lord Jesus.

PRAYER AND MINISTRY TIME

Remember to choose a person who will receive prayer and ministry for this lesson. Help the children record this person's name in their Workbook. You should each agree to ask God to tell you something that will encourage that person. Refer to the prayer and ministry section of the Introduction, as needed.

Hearing God Through the Loud Voice of the Holy Spirit

TEACHING CONTENT

1. *Say*: We have been learning about the many ways that we can hear God's voice.

    Ask: Can you name some of the ways for me?
    [We have talked about hearing from God through His written Word—the Bible, an inner knowing, and the soft, inner voice.]

    Say: Once in a while God speaks to us in a loud voice using words. It can also be called the authoritative voice. "Authoritative" describes a person who is in charge. God, who is our Boss, and who is in charge of our lives, sometimes sends a very clear message by speaking loudly. It seems so loud that we think people around us can hear it too, but they can't. The Holy Spirit speaks these loud words in our spirit.

    God may speak to us in His loud voice to give us a **WARNING**, in order to protect us. He will use His loud voice to get our attention. God may speak to us in His loud voice to give us important **INSTRUCTIONS**. Remember when God spoke to Noah? He gave Noah exact directions on how to build the ark. God probably used His loud voice so that Noah would build a ship that could save his family and all those animals. God may use His loud voice to send us in a certain **DIRECTION.** His loud, authoritative voice can help us move in a life-changing direction. Our Father cares about every part of our life, including the direction our life is taking.

    Ask: Have you ever heard God speaking to you with His loud voice?
    If so, what did God say?

2. *Say*: A boy named Samuel heard God's loud, authoritative voice. Samuel was around 12 years old.[1] He lived with a priest named Eli in the town of Shiloh. Samuel served God by living and working in the place of worship called the Tent of Meeting. His story is found in **1 Samuel 3.**

    Help the children find and read aloud **1 Samuel 3:1-5.**
    > **The boy Samuel served the Lord under the direction of Eli. In those days the Lord didn't give many messages to his people. He didn't give them many visions.**
    > **One night Eli was lying down in his usual place. His eyes were becoming so weak he couldn't see very well. Samuel was lying down in the Lord's house. That's where the ark of God was kept. The lamp of God was still burning. The Lord called out to Samuel.**
    > **Samuel answered, "Here I am." He ran over to Eli and said, "Here I am. You called out to me."**
    > **But Eli said, "I didn't call you. Go back and lie down." So he went and lay down.**

    Say: Samuel was sleeping in the Tent of Meeting, and he thought that Eli had called him. Samuel's job was to help Eli, the old priest who couldn't see very well. (See the Study Notes at the end of this lesson for more explanation.) God's voice seemed very loud to Samuel. It woke him up. God's voice was very clear, but no one else heard the voice because it was inside Samuel's spirit.

    Samuel did not recognize the Lord's voice because he had never heard His voice before. Samuel did not have much chance to watch other people hearing from God either. Eli was a sinful priest, who did not want to be obedient to God. So, God was not saying much to Eli. It is encouraging to know that Samuel, who became such a great man of God, started out having no experience in hearing God's voice. So, all of us have the chance to hear God's voice more and more clearly.

3. *Find and read aloud* **1 Samuel 3:6-9.**

> **Again the Lord called out, "Samuel!" Samuel got up and went to Eli. He said, "Here I am. You called out to me."**
>
> **"My son," Eli said, "I didn't call you. Go back and lie down." Samuel didn't know the Lord yet. That's because the Lord still hadn't given him a message.**
>
> **The Lord called out for the third time. He said, "Samuel!" Samuel got up and went to Eli. He said, "Here I am. You called out to me."**
>
> **Then Eli realized that the Lord was calling the boy. So Eli told Samuel, "Go and lie down. If someone calls out to you again, say, 'Speak, Lord. I'm listening.'" So Samuel went and lay down in his place.**

Ask: How would you feel if God used His loud voice to speak to you?

Say: Samuel may have been excited and nervous all at once. He may have been surprised that the Lord wanted to speak to him, a child.

LA #1

4. *Find and read aloud* **1 Samuel 3:10-14.**

> **The Lord came and stood there. He called out, just as he had done the other times. He said, "Samuel! Samuel!"**
>
> **Then Samuel replied, "Speak. I'm listening.'"**
>
> **The Lord said to Samuel, "Pay attention! I am about to do something terrible in Israel. It will make the ears of everyone who hears about it tingle. At that time I will do everything to Eli and his family that I said I would. I will finish what I have started. I told Eli I would punish his family forever. He knew his sons were sinning. He knew they were saying bad things about me. In spite of that, he did not stop them. So I made a promise to the family of Eli. I said, 'The sins of Eli's family will never be paid for by bringing sacrifices or offerings.'"**

Say: What God said to Samuel really was a new direction! The Lord gave Samuel a special job to do—to give an important message to Eli. God did not want Samuel and His people to be like the disobedient priest and his wicked sons. The Lord was also sending Eli a strong message. God let Eli know that He would not let Eli's family get away with such sinful behavior.

Ask: How would you feel if you were Samuel, and God gave you this bad news to give to Eli?
[Samuel was probably scared. He probably didn't want to tell Eli this bad news.]

5. *Find and read aloud* **1 Samuel 3:15-18.**

> **Samuel lay down until morning. Then he opened the doors of the Lord's house. He was afraid to tell Eli about the vision he had received. But Eli called out to him. He said, "Samuel, my son."**
>
> **Samuel answered, "Here I am."**
>
> **"What did the Lord say to you?" Eli asked. "Don't hide from me anything he told you. If you do, may God punish you greatly." So Samuel told him everything. He didn't hide anything from him. Then Eli said, "He is the Lord. Let him do what he thinks is best."**

Say: In **verse 15** it says that Samuel received a **VISION**. You may remember that in the book *Is That Really You, God?* Loren had a vision that was like a mental movie, pictures in his mind. So, in the vision that Samuel received, he must have seen God come and talk to him in the loud, authoritative voice. Thankfully, Eli did not get angry with Samuel! Eli must have thought that if God said it, there was nothing he could do.

6. *Find and read aloud* **1 Samuel 3:19 through 1 Samuel 4:1.**

> **As Samuel grew up, the Lord was with him. He made everything Samuel said come true. So all the Israelites recognized that Samuel really was a prophet of the Lord. Everyone from Dan all the way to Beersheba knew it. The Lord continued to appear at Shiloh. There he made himself known to Samuel through the messages he gave him. And Samuel gave those messages to all the Israelites.**

Say: In **verse 21** we read that God continued to be with Samuel and speak to him. Sometimes the Lord would give Samuel messages to pass on to the Israelites. Samuel became a great priest, prophet and judge who loved and honored God. Even though Samuel did not recognize God's voice at first, God did not quit calling him. Our God is patient and will give us practice in learning to recognize His voice.

LA #2, AP #1

7. *Say:* Other examples in Scripture of the loud, authoritative voice include the following passages.

Find and read aloud **Exodus 3:4.**
> **"The Lord saw that Moses had gone over to look. So God spoke to him from inside the bush. He called out, 'Moses! Moses!'**
> **'Here I am,' Moses said."**

Find and read aloud **Genesis 6:12-14.**
> **God saw how sinful the earth had become. All its people were living very sinful lives. So God said to Noah, "I am going to put an end to everyone. They have filled the earth with their harmful acts. I am certainly going to destroy them and the earth. So make yourself an ark out of cypress wood. Make rooms in it. Cover it with tar inside and out."**

Find and read aloud **Mark 9:7.**
> **"Then a cloud appeared and covered them. A voice came from the cloud. It said, 'This is my Son, and I love him. Listen to him!'"**

Find and read aloud **Acts 9:3-5.**
> **On his journey, Saul approached Damascus. Suddenly a light from heaven flashed around him. He fell to the ground. He heard a voice speak to him, "Saul! Saul! Why are you opposing me?"**
> **"Who are you, Lord?" Saul asked.**
> **"I am Jesus," he replied. "I am the one you are opposing."**

8. God does not speak to us in the loud, authoritative voice of the Holy Spirit very often. Because the Lord is our Boss, He gets to choose the best way to speak with us.

LA #3, LA #4

PRAYER AND MINISTRY TIME:

Take turns sharing what the Lord has given you to share with the person receiving ministry. Allow time now to hear anything more that the Lord wants to say.

Review the Prayer and Ministry Time section of the Introduction, as needed.

LEARNING ACTIVITIES

Activity #1 Eating something black and white

MATERIALS NEEDED: Vanilla and chocolate sandwich cookies, or vanilla and chocolate pudding

Say: Samuel heard God's loud voice during the night. God is with us during the day and the night, and He can speak to us any time. God is with us during the day and the night. This vanilla cookie (or pudding) represents the daytime, and the chocolate cookie (or pudding) represents the nighttime.

Say: Let's find and read aloud what the psalm writer wrote to God in **Psalm 139:9-12:**
Suppose I were to rise with the sun in the east.
> **Suppose I travel to the west where it sinks into the ocean.**
Your hand would always be there to guide me.
> **Your right hand would still be holding me close.**
Suppose I were to say, "I'm sure the darkness will hide me.
> **The light around me will become as dark as night."**
Even that darkness would not be dark to you.
> **The night would shine like the day,**
because darkness is like light to you.

Say: The Lord can speak to us at any time. We can pray to Him any time, day or night. *Read aloud* **Psalm 55:17: "Evening, morning and noon I groan and cry out. And he hears my voice."**

Have the children write out **Psalm 139:9-12** in their Workbook.

Ask: Have you sensed God speaking to you more during the day or at night?
Have them describe a time when they sensed God speaking to them at night.

Activity #2 Identifying familiar loud sounds

MATERIALS NEEDED: A tape recorder or recording application on a smart phone

Before playing: Record all kinds of loud sounds and voices that are familiar to the children, both difficult and easy to recognize. As you begin playing each recorded sound, have the children listen carefully. When someone recognizes what the sound is, he should name it.

After playing, have the children list in their Workbook the names of sounds that they recognized.

Activity #3 Play "Follow God's Voice."

MATERIALS NEEDED: A blindfold and a treat to eat

Blindfold the player. Place a treat to eat at the end of an obstacle course. Place obstacles in the child's path. Tell him that you will play "God" and give him directions in the loud, authoritative voice, to help him avoid hitting the obstacles. Help the child to move safely through the course by giving clear, concise directions. Tell him when to move forward and when to turn right or left. If he hits an obstacle, he needs to go back to the beginning and start again. Continue until he has reached the snack. The children can take turns being "God" and giving loud directions.

For older children, you can make it more challenging by having three different people giving the player different directions. He must recognize and follow only "God's" voice.

After playing, have the children describe in their Workbook what it was like to play this game. They are asked the questions: Were you able to get through the obstacle course without running into anything? Was it difficult following the directions exactly? Do you think you would be able to obey God if He spoke to you in His loud, authoritative voice?

Activity #4 Listen to Songs About Hearing From God
MATERIALS NEEDED: A phone or computer with internet access

Search YouTube for the song "Speak, O Lord – Keith and Kristyn Getty." Also search YouTube for the song "Speak to Me, Lord" by Rebecca St. James. Ask the children to choose which of these two songs is better at saying what is in their heart?

You could begin the prayer and ministry time by listening to one of these songs. You could also play the songs while the children work on an art project.

ART PROJECTS

Project #1 Young Samuel hears the authoritative voice of God.
MATERIALS NEEDED: Lesson 11 Samuel coloring picture, crayons, black tempera paint and brushes

To prevent water damage, make a copy of the Lesson 11 coloring page of Samuel. Have the children color that copy using crayons. Have them lightly brush over their pictures with watered-down black tempera paint, creating a nighttime effect.

STUDY NOTES

The NIV Study Bible footnote states, "Samuel is now no longer a little child. The Jewish historian Josephus places his age at 12 years; he may have been older."[1] The Ark of the Covenant was a wooden box covered with gold. The box had a pure gold cover called the mercy seat. On the mercy seat were two golden angels whose wings stretched over the mercy seat. God had commanded Moses to have an artisan make the Ark of the Covenant (**Exodus 25:10-22; Exodus 37:1-9**). Moses placed inside it the two stone tablets with the Ten Commandments carved on them. Later, two other items were also placed in the Ark: Aaron's rod that budded (**Numbers 17:10**) and a jar that held manna given by God while His people traveled in the wilderness (**Exodus 16:33; Hebrews 9:4**). The Israelites were careful to protect and keep the Ark of the Covenant because God promised to meet them there.

The lamp of God used then was a seven-branched candlestick filled with oil. It was kept lit all night in the Tent of Meeting. It may have been Samuel's job to make sure the lamp stayed lit during the night.

LESSON 12

GOD HAS MANY DIFFERENT WAYS

OBJECTIVE

God has many different ways of guiding us. We know that God does what is best. He may choose to guide us in a simple way or in an exciting, dramatic way. We leave it up to Him to decide how He will speak to us.

GOD HAS MANY DIFFERENT WAYS

LESSON 12 CONTENT OBJECTIVE

To understand that God has many different ways of guiding us. We know that God does what is best. He may choose to guide us in a simple way or in an exciting, dramatic way. We leave it up to Him to decide how He will speak to us.

LESSON 12 KEY SCRIPTURE

Each day read aloud this lesson's scripture. Have the children write it out in the Workbook in the space provided. Encourage them to memorize this lesson's verse by the end of the week. Challenge the children to recite it without reading it.

Isaiah 55:8-9 "'My thoughts are not like your thoughts. And your ways are not like my ways,' announces the Lord. 'The heavens are higher than the earth. And my ways are higher than your ways. My thoughts are higher than your thoughts.'"

LESSON 12 READING ASSIGNMENT

Read Chapters 17 and 18 in *Is That Really You, God?*
Some children will need you to read portions of the assigned reading to them, others can read the chapters on their own or take turns reading aloud as a group.

TEACHING CONTENT, LEARNING ACTIVITIES AND ART PROJECTS

These are the largest components of the lesson. Depending upon your children's ages, you will need to decide how much of each section to cover in any given day. Select Learning Activities and Art Projects that fit your children's abilities and interests. Feel free to be creative and have fun as you lead your children into a real relationship with the Lord Jesus.

PRAYER AND MINISTRY TIME

Remember to choose a person who will receive prayer and ministry for this lesson. Help the children record this person's name in their Workbook. You should each agree to ask God to tell you something that will encourage that person. Refer to the prayer and ministry section of the Introduction, as needed.

God Has Many Different Ways

TEACHING CONTENT

Different Ways God Speaks

1. *Ask*: What are some of the ways God speaks to us that we have already learned about?
   [We can hear God through the Bible, an inner knowing, a soft, inner voice or a loud, authoritative voice.]

   Say: Today we will learn about more ways that God speaks. But first, let's talk about what God is like.

2. *Help the children find and read aloud* **Isaiah 55:8-9.**
   > **"My thoughts are not like your thoughts.**
   > **And your ways are not like my ways,"**
   > announces the Lord.
   > **"The heavens are higher than the earth.**
   > **And my ways are higher than your ways.**
   > **My thoughts are higher than your thoughts."**

   Say: God is very different from us. He is one of a kind; there is no one like Him! He is so different from us that the things He will do or say may surprise us or be different than we expect.

3. Here are some different ways that God spoke to people in the Bible.

   a. *Find and read aloud* **Luke 2:8-14.**
      > There were shepherds living out in the fields nearby. It was night, and they were taking care of their sheep. An angel of the Lord appeared to them. And the glory of the Lord shone around them. They were terrified. But the angel said to them, "Do not be afraid. I bring you good news. It will bring great joy for all the people. Today in the town of David a Savior has been born to you. He is the Messiah, the Lord. Here is how you will know I am telling you the truth. You will find a baby wrapped in strips of cloth and lying in a manger."
      > Suddenly a large group of angels from heaven also appeared. They were praising God. They said, "May glory be given to God in the highest heaven!
      > And may peace be given to those he is pleased with on earth!"

   Say: God can speak to people through ANGELS. One time was when Jesus was born.

   Ask: Do you know anyone who has seen an angel?

   Say: If you see one, you know that God has sent him to get something done.

   b. *Find and read aloud* **Matthew 2:13.**
      > "When the Wise Men had left, Joseph had a dream. In the dream an angel of the Lord appeared to Joseph. 'Get up!' the angel said. 'Take the child and his mother and escape to Egypt. Stay there until I tell you to come back. Herod is going to search for the child. He wants to kill him.'"

   Say: God also speaks to people through DREAMS. These verses tell about when Jesus' father, Joseph, was told to go to Egypt, to protect Jesus and His family.

Ask: Has God ever given you a spiritual dream, to tell you something?

c.   *Find and read aloud* **Acts 16:9-10.**

> **During the night Paul had a vision. He saw a man from Macedonia standing and begging him. "Come over to Macedonia!" the man said. "Help us!" After Paul had seen the vision, we got ready at once to leave for Macedonia. We decided that God had called us to preach the good news there.**

Say: God can give us a message through a VISION. In these verses, Paul was shown in a vision to go to a different place to preach.

Sometimes it is a quick picture of something in our mind. When we ask God about the picture, He may tell us what He is saying. A vision can also be like having a dream but we are awake, like a movie in our mind.

Ask: Have you ever had a vision—either a mental movie or a quick picture in your mind?

Say: Here is a story from a 13-year-old girl named Naomi, who was studying this lesson:

> During the week when I was studying visions, I misplaced my Kindle. I am an avid reader, and I was disappointed I couldn't finish the book I was reading. I looked all over my house for my Kindle but I couldn't find it anywhere. One night, about three days after I lost it, I was laying in my bed and I decided to pray to God and ask where it was. As I lay there in silence, a picture came into my mind. It was an image of the bookshelf in my mom and dad's room. I thought it was weird that the image kept coming to my mind. The next morning, I went to my mom's room and looked for it throughout the shelves. I couldn't find my Kindle anywhere, but I did find a paperback copy of the book I had been reading, so I started reading the paperback version. After about five minutes of reading the paperback copy, my sister called me. She had found my Kindle! She said it was on top of the book-shelf buried under some papers. I knew God had shown me that image and guided me to what had been lost!

d.   *Find and read aloud* **1 Samuel 3:11-14.**

> **The Lord said to Samuel, "Pay attention! I am about to do something terrible in Israel. It will make the ears of everyone who hears about it tingle. At that time I will do everything to Eli and his family that I said I would. I will finish what I have started. I told Eli I would punish his family forever. He knew his sons were sinning. He knew they were saying bad things about me. In spite of that, he did not stop them. So I made a promise to the family of Eli. I said, 'The sins of Eli's family will never be paid for by bringing sacrifices or offerings.'"**

Say: God can speak to you through the WORDS OF OTHER PEOPLE. This was a passage we read in Lesson 11 when God wanted to give a message to Eli. God spoke to Eli, the priest, through Samuel, the child. God gave Samuel a special message to tell Eli.

God can give a special message to a person so that he will know what God is thinking. It is called *a word of knowledge*. (Parents/Teachers, see the Study Notes below.) With a word of knowledge, God can tell a person something that only God knows, something that will help them. For us, the words would be something a person says that you feel in your spirit is true and important.

Ask: Do you remember a time when God spoke to you through the words of another person?

LA #1, LA #2, AP #1, AP #2

God speaks so that all people can come to Him.

1. *Find and read aloud* **Acts 8:1-3.**

   On that day the church in Jerusalem began to be attacked and treated badly. All except the apostles were scattered throughout Judea and Samaria. Godly Jews buried Stephen. They mourned deeply for him. But Saul began to destroy the church. He went from house to house. He dragged away men and women and put them in prison.

   Say: When the believers in Jerusalem were treated very badly, many moved from the area. Wherever the believers went, they carried the good news about Jesus with them. Because of this, the number of Christians actually grew! This made the Jewish leaders really mad. They gave Saul permission to go from house to house and to drag believing men and women off to prison.

2. *Find and read aloud* **Acts 9:3-7.**

   On his journey, Saul approached Damascus. Suddenly a light from heaven flashed around him. He fell to the ground. He heard a voice speak to him, "Saul! Saul! Why are you opposing me?"

   "Who are you, Lord?" Saul asked.

   "I am Jesus," he replied. "I am the one you are opposing. Now get up and go into the city. There you will be told what you must do."

   The men traveling with Saul stood there. They weren't able to speak. They had heard the sound. But they didn't see anyone.

   Ask: How did God get Saul's attention?

   [God caused a bright light to flash around Saul, and Saul fell to the ground. Then God spoke to him using his loud, authoritative voice.]

   Say: God's power and presence has made other people fall to the ground (**John 18:5-6; Revelation 1:17**). When that happens, God is saying, "Hello! I am God, and I am here!" Jesus thinks that if you are treating His followers badly, then you are treating **HIM** badly. He sees us as His body on earth. God was changing Saul's mind about throwing believers in prison. God was changing the direction of Saul's life.

3. *Find and read aloud* **Acts 9:8-9.**

   "Saul got up from the ground. He opened his eyes, but he couldn't see. So they led him by the hand into Damascus. For three days he was blind. He didn't eat or drink anything."

   Ask: Why do you think that Saul didn't eat or drink anything for three days?

   How would you feel if you suddenly became blind?

   How would you feel if you heard God say those words in **Acts 9:3-7** to you?

4. *Find and read aloud* **Acts 9:10-16.**

   In Damascus there was a believer named Ananias. The Lord called out to him in a vision. "Ananias!" he said.

   "Yes, Lord," he answered.

   The Lord told him, "Go to the house of Judas on Straight Street. Ask for a man

from Tarsus named Saul. He is praying. In a vision Saul has seen a man come and place his hands on him. That man's name is Ananias. In the vision, Ananias placed his hands on Saul so he could see again."

"Lord," Ananias answered, "I've heard many reports about this man. They say he has done great harm to your holy people in Jerusalem. Now he has come here to arrest all those who worship you. The chief priests have given him authority to do this."

But the Lord said to Ananias, "Go! I have chosen this man to work for me. He will announce my name to the Gentiles and to their kings. He will also announce my name to the people of Israel. I will show him how much he must suffer for me."

Ask: How did God communicate with Ananias?
[The Lord called out to Ananias in a vision.]

Say: During that vision, God said he would also give Saul a vision of Ananias helping him see again. God also gave Ananias a word of knowledge about Saul. God told Ananias something that only God knew—that in the future Saul would tell many people about Jesus, both Jews and Gentiles and their kings.

It might have seemed dangerous for Ananias to go to that house because Saul's friends were there. They could have caused problems for the believers. However, God's words about what He was doing in Saul's life made Ananias brave. He decided to trust God and obey Him.

Ask: Why do you think God gave Saul that vision in **Acts 9:11-12**?
What do you think He was saying to Saul?
[Maybe God was saying, "Don't worry; you will be able to see again. I am sending someone here who has my power to heal your eyes. You can trust him. I have a job for you to do."]

5. *Find and read aloud* **Acts 9:17-20.**
Then Ananias went to the house and entered it. He placed his hands on Saul. "Brother Saul," he said, "you saw the Lord Jesus. He appeared to you on the road as you were coming here. He has sent me so that you will be able to see again. You will be filled with the Holy Spirit." Right away something like scales fell from Saul's eyes. And he could see again. He got up and was baptized. After eating some food, he got his strength back.
Saul spent several days with the believers in Damascus. Right away he began to preach in the synagogues. He taught that Jesus was the Son of God.

Say: Ananias placed his hands on Saul and prayed that the Holy Spirit would fill him. Saul would need the power and help from the Holy Spirit to do the job God was giving him. God gave Ananias a gift of healing for Saul (**1 Corinthians 12:9**). Saul's eyes were healed and he was eager to be baptized in the name of Jesus.

Saul then spent time with the other believers in Damascus—not to hurt them, but to strengthen their faith by sharing his story. Now Saul understood the scriptures and what they said about Jesus. He probably heard many stories about Jesus from the believers as well!

Say: God is looking for people who are like Saul, willing to do God's work.

Ask: Are you willing to be such a person?
Are you willing to answer if God calls you to tell people about Jesus?

6. In this passage, God used many different ways to speak to His people.
   a. Saul saw the light from heaven, fell to the ground and heard Jesus' voice.
   b. Ananias was given a vision and a word of knowledge about Saul.
   c. Saul had a vision of Ananias coming to lay hands on him.
   d. God gave Ananias a gift of healing for Saul.

   Ask: Why was God so generous with all these ways for them to hear His voice?

   [God spoke in all these different ways to bring Saul to faith in Jesus, so that he could announce who Jesus is to the Gentiles and the people of Israel. God wants all people to have forgiveness of their sins and to hear His voice!]

7. *Find and read aloud* Joel 2:28-29.
   "I will pour out my Spirit on all people. Your sons and daughters will prophesy, your old men will dream dreams, your young men will see visions. Even on my servants, both men and women, I will pour out my Spirit in those days."

   Say: This prophecy started coming true at Pentecost when God sent the Holy Spirit to Jesus' followers. Before that, the Holy Spirit only rested on special people like kings, priests, prophets or judges. Today, the Holy Spirit is still pouring out on people—young, old, boys and girls, in order to help us hear what God is saying to us.

8. *Say*: As we seek God, study His Word, and keep our hearts soft towards Him, God will choose how He speaks to each of us. Our responsibility is to spend time with God and to do what the Holy Spirit asks us to do.

   LA #3, LA #4, AP #3

PRAYER AND MINISTRY TIME:

Take turns sharing what the Lord has given you to say to the person receiving ministry.
Allow time now to hear anything more that the Lord wants to say.

Review the Prayer and Ministry Time section of the Introduction, as needed.

LEARNING ACTIVITIES

Activity #1 Worship God for His greatness and creativity in speaking to us.
MATERIALS NEEDED: A Bible

Spend time praising the Lord together. In order for the worship to be heart-felt, have the children list all the wonderful things God has done in their life lately. Encourage them to list God's characteristics, what He is like. Encourage them to list places in nature where they see God's creativity.

Then, verbally praise the Lord for who He is and what He has done. Encourage the children to tell the Lord their thoughts about Him. For example, they could tell the Lord, "God, You are a great God! You are mighty! You are wonderful! I love how you gave zebras stripes! Thank You for providing everything I need. Lord, I praise You! Lord, I love You!"

Or instead, the children could express their admiration for God by reading aloud a favorite psalm, or read **Psalm 150** together and praise the Lord! If you choose this option, have the children write in their Workbook which psalm they chose and which verses they like best.

Activity #2 A Rap Song
MATERIALS NEEDED: A phone or computer with internet access

Search YouTube for a rap song that talks about hearing from God. To find an example, type in "MC Jin – Over the Edge ft. Dawen music video." Help the children learn and perform this song or one they like. Or instead, they could write additional verses to the song and write them in their Workbook. Alternatively, they could simply identify the parts when the rapper mentions God speaking to him.

Activity #3 Watch a video about how Paul came to believe in Jesus.
MATERIALS NEEDED: A phone or computer with internet access

Search YouTube for a video titled "Paul's Ministry Saddleback Kids" and watch it together.

Activity #4 Visions in the Bible
MATERIALS NEEDED: A Bible

Have the children read in the Bible about other times that God used visions to speak to people. Have them read **Isaiah 6:1-8** and **Revelation 1:12-17** and write what happened in these visions in their Workbook.

ART PROJECTS

Project #1 God speaks to us through dreams.
MATERIALS NEEDED: Paper, marker, crayons or paint and brushes

Ask: Has God ever given you a dream that might be telling you something?

Say: If so, draw a picture of what God showed you. Write out in your Workbook what you think the Lord was saying to you through the dream.

Project #2 God speaks through visions.
MATERIALS NEEDED: Paper, markers, crayons or paint and brushes

Have the children draw or paint a picture of one of the visions described in the Bible. Some accounts of visions can be found at **Acts 16:9-10; Isaiah 6:1-8** and **Revelation 1:12-17**.

Project #3 Illustrate the Scriptures.
MATERIALS NEEDED: Clay or play-dough, paper, watercolors, brushes, markers, colored pencils, magazine pages, scissors, glue, cardboard, Scotch tape

Our God is creative, and He uses many creative ways to speak to us. He has given us the ability to be creative also. Provide various mediums for the children to use for an art project. The children should create something that represents a scene from one of the Bible passages you read in this lesson. They could use clay or play-dough to re-create a character, make a picture of a scene in a passage, make a collage that expresses an idea in that passage from magazine pictures and words, create a diorama of that passage, etc.

STUDY NOTES:

Manifestation Gifts of the Holy Spirit

Sometimes God speaks to us in a special way through a manifestation gift, as the Holy Spirit moves upon a believer to speak a word to someone else. We have included definitions of some of the manifestation gifts that operate this way.

A *word of knowledge* is one of the manifestations of the Holy Spirit mentioned in **1 Corinthians 12:7-11**. Dick Iverson in his book *The Holy Spirit Today* explains:

> "The *'word of knowledge'* is the supernatural revelation to man of some detail of the knowledge of God. It is the impartation of facts and information which are humanly impossible to know." It is knowledge that is a portion of God's knowledge of facts of the past, present or future. It may reveal the whereabouts of men, warn of coming danger, or expose hypocrisy.[1]

A *word of wisdom* is another manifestation of the Holy Spirit. Here is a definition:

> "The gift of the *word of wisdom* is supernaturally given by God. It is not *'a'* word of wisdom but *'the'* word of wisdom. It is not just a word on the subject or situation at hand, it is the word on it. It is the answer or solution or the will of God in that situation."[2]

LESSON 13

GO AND TELL

OBJECTIVE

It is very important that we tell other people about Jesus and what He has done for us. We want them to hear God's voice and to have Him as their Shepherd. We want them to have eternal life too! If we are willing to follow what the Holy Spirit tells us to do, He will lead us to people He has made ready to hear about Jesus. We need to persistently pray for the people in our lives who don't believe in Him, loving them with Jesus' love.

GO AND TELL

LESSON 13 CONTENT OBJECTIVE

To understand that it is very important that we tell other people about Jesus and what He has done for us. We want them to hear God's voice and to have Him as their Shepherd. We want them to have eternal life too! If we are willing to follow what the Holy Spirit tells us to do, He will lead us to people He has made ready to hear about Jesus. We need to persistently pray for the people in our lives who don't believe in Him, loving them with Jesus' love.

LESSON 13 KEY SCRIPTURES

Each day read aloud this lesson's scriptures. Have the children write out one of them in the Workbook in the space provided. Encourage them to memorize one of this lesson's verses by the end of the week. Challenge the children to recite it without reading it.

Matthew 28:19-20 "So you must go and make disciples of all nations. Baptize them in the name of the Father and of the Son and of the Holy Spirit. Teach them to obey everything I have commanded you. And you can be sure that I am always with you, to the very end."

Younger children may want to learn this shorter verse:
Mark 16:15 "He said to them, 'Go into all the world. Preach the good news to everyone.'"

LESSON 13 READING ASSIGNMENT

Read Chapters 19, 20 and Twelve Points to Remember in *Is That Really You, God?*
Some children will need you to read portions of the assigned reading to them, others can read the chapters on their own or take turns reading aloud as a group.

TEACHING CONTENT, LEARNING ACTIVITIES AND ART PROJECTS

These are the largest components of the lesson. Depending upon your children's ages, you will need to decide how much of each section to cover in any given day. Select Learning Activities and Art Projects that fit your children's abilities and interests. Feel free to be creative and have fun as you lead your children into a real relationship with the Lord Jesus.

PRAYER AND MINISTRY TIME

The prayer and ministry time will be different this lesson. Refer to the prayer and ministry section at the end of this lesson.

Go and Tell!

TEACHING CONTENT

1. *Ask*: If someone asked you "Does God speak to you?" what would you say?

   Say: Tell me about a time God gave you direction or helped you by saying something to you. *Allow the children to share some of their experiences.*

2. Help the children find and read aloud **Mark 16:15.**
   "He said to them, 'Go into all the world. Preach the good news to everyone.'"

   Say: Before Jesus went back to heaven, He told His disciples that this was their job. When we tell others about what God has done in our life and that Jesus died to pay the price for our sin, we are telling them the good news about Jesus.

3. *Find and read aloud* **Matthew 28:19-20.**
   "So you must go and make disciples of all nations. Baptize them in the name of the Father and of the Son and of the Holy Spirit. Teach them to obey everything I have commanded you. And you can be sure that I am always with you, to the very end."

   Say: From the beginning of time, God had a plan to send Jesus to earth to be our Shepherd. God knew that we would often make wrong choices and sin against Him. So He sent His Son Jesus, to live as a man but then die, to pay the penalty for our sins. When Jesus was ready to go back to heaven, He knew that He needed to leave followers who would tell other people about Him.

4. *Say*: We are going to read about the time that Jesus called Simon Peter, James and John to be His followers. In the days before this, Jesus had been healing many sick people. This day, a big crowd wanted to hear what Jesus had to say.

   Find and read aloud **Luke 5:1-3:**
   > **One day Jesus was standing by the Sea of Galilee. The people crowded around him and listened to the word of God. Jesus saw two boats at the edge of the water. They had been left there by the fishermen, who were washing their nets. He got into the boat that belonged to Simon. Jesus asked him to go out a little way from shore. Then he sat down in the boat and taught the people.**

   Ask: Why do you think Jesus decided to get into the boat?
   [One reason may have been that the large group of listeners was crowding too close. Or maybe Jesus got into a boat so that He could sit down. Maybe He did so that the people at the back of the crowd could hear Him better, because the sound of voices carries farther over water.]

5. *Find and read aloud* **Luke 5:4-5.**
   > **When he finished speaking, he turned to Simon. Jesus said, "Go out into deep water. Let down the nets so you can catch some fish."**
   > **Simon answered, "Master, we've worked hard all night and haven't caught anything. But because you say so, I will let down the nets."**

Say: Peter was an experienced fisherman. He made his living by catching fish. If Peter was unable to catch any fish the night before, then no one could have! But, Jesus told him to let down his nets again. Even though Peter was probably really tired, he did what Jesus told him because he knew that this man, Jesus, was very special.

6. *Find and read aloud* **Luke 5:6-7.**

> **When they had done so, they caught a large number of fish. There were so many that their nets began to break. So they motioned to their partners in the other boat to come and help them. They came and filled both boats so full that they began to sink.**
>
> **When Simon Peter saw this, he fell at Jesus' knees. "Go away from me, Lord!" he said. "I am a sinful man!" He and everyone with him were amazed at the number of fish they had caught. So were James and John, the sons of Zebedee, who worked with Simon.**
>
> **Then Jesus said to Simon, "Don't be afraid. From now on you will fish for people." So they pulled their boats up on shore. Then they left everything and followed him.**

Ask: Was Peter surprised that they caught so many fish?
  Why did they catch fish this time, when they had not caught any fish after trying all night?
[Because they did what Jesus told them to do, and God brought the fish to them.]

Ask: What did Jesus tell them that they would fish for from now on?
[They would fish for people!]

Ask: How can you be a fisher of people?
[Use Jesus as the bait! Tell them about Jesus so they will come to Him.]

Ask: Do you think it is important to listen to God's voice in order to be a fisher of people?
  What might happen to us if we tried to tell others about Jesus all by ourselves, without listening to God and doing what He tells us to do?
[We might come back with empty nets, that is, the people might not decide to believe in Jesus.]

Say: As we listen to and obey God's voice, our nets can be full, and WE can be fishers of people.

LA #1, AP #1

Three Followers of Jesus

1. *Say*: Next we will read about three followers of Jesus, who later became fishers of people. It was now three years later, and Jesus had been killed and his body was laid in a tomb. These three followers went to Jesus' tomb. They were very sad that Jesus had been killed and they missed Him.

Find and read aloud **John 20:1-7.**

> **Early on the first day of the week, Mary Magdalene went to the tomb. It was still dark. She saw that the stone had been moved away from the entrance. So she ran to Simon Peter and another disciple, the one Jesus loved. She said, "They have taken the Lord out of the tomb! We don't know where they have put him!"**
>
> **So Peter and the other disciple started out for the tomb. Both of them were running. The other disciple ran faster than Peter. He reached the tomb first. He bent over and looked in at the strips of linen lying there. But he did not go in. Then Simon Peter came along behind him. He went straight into the tomb. He saw the strips of linen lying there. He also saw the funeral cloth that had been wrapped around Jesus' head. The cloth was still lying in its place. It was separate from the linen.**

Say: Mary, Peter and the other disciple did not know for sure what had happened to Jesus' body. The man running to the tomb ahead of Peter was John. He wrote these verses and called himself "another disciple, the one Jesus loved."

2. *Say*: **LET'S FIRST LOOK AT PETER.** We know Simon Peter was a fisherman and that he left everything to follow Jesus. What you may not know is what Jesus said to Peter at the Last Supper before He was arrested.

3. *Find and read aloud* **Luke 22:31-32.**
"Simon, Simon! Satan has asked to sift all of you disciples like wheat. But I have prayed for you, Simon. I have prayed that your faith will not fail. When you have turned back, help your brothers to be strong."

Say: Jesus called Peter "Simon" three times in these verses. This was his old name. Jesus had already changed his name to Peter. Peter means rock, and this showed Peter how Jesus saw him—that he would become a strong person whom others could depend on. The name Simon stood for his old, sinful nature. Jesus knew that Peter's sinful nature would cause him to act like a coward.

4. *Find and read aloud* **Luke 22:33-34.**
"But Simon replied, 'Lord, I am ready to go with you to prison and to death.' Jesus answered, 'I tell you, Peter, you will say three times that you don't know me. And you will do it before the rooster crows today.'"

Say: Peter did not like hearing that he would not be a good friend to Jesus! Peter was usually very quick to act, but sometimes he was impulsive and spoke before he thought. In **verse 33** Peter insisted that Jesus was wrong. Then in **verse 34** Jesus said what would ACTUALLY happen—that Peter would say he didn't even know Jesus. Notice that Jesus called him Peter here, maybe to give him hope that he would become strong.

Everything turned out as Jesus had said it would. When Jesus was arrested and was being questioned, Peter denied that he knew Jesus—three times. Peter lied because he was afraid that he also would get arrested (**Luke 22:54-62**).

5. *Say*: Thankfully, God doesn't look at what we DO as much as He looks at what we INTEND TO DO in our hearts. Jesus knew that Simon Peter would fail, but He also knew that Peter would repent (turn away from this sin) and eventually be a strong leader for the other followers.

> A lesson from Peter's life is: **IT IS BETTER TO BE A FOLLOWER AND FAIL, THAN ONE WHO FAILS TO FOLLOW.**

Even when we mess up, Jesus is quick to forgive us. He tells us that when we have repented (turned away from our sin), we should go ahead and do what He has told us to do.

6. *Say*: **LET'S GO BACK TO JESUS' EMPTY TOMB AND LOOK AT THE DISCIPLE JOHN NOW.** He was the one who ran fast and reached the tomb first. John was one of Peter's friends. He helped haul in the big catch of fish. He heard Jesus' call to be fishers of people.

Ask: Why do you think John called himself **"the one Jesus loved"** in **John 20:2**?

Does Jesus love one of His followers more than the others?

[No! God does not love one of His children more than another. Scripture says that God **"treats everyone the same"** Deuteronomy 10:17 (See also **2 Chronicles 19:7**.)]

Say: John called himself **"the one Jesus loved"** because he TRUSTED that Jesus loved him. He ACCEPTED Jesus' love in the same way we would accept a gift given to us.

7. *Find and read aloud* **John 20:8-10**.
"The disciple who had reached the tomb first also went inside. He saw and believed. They still did not understand from Scripture that Jesus had to rise from the dead. Then the disciples went back to where they were staying."

Say: **Verse 8** says that John **"saw and believed."** Maybe he remembered what Jesus had said—that He would be raised from the dead (**Matthew 20:18-19**). Even though John didn't fully understand, he was ready to believe because he had a soft heart. He and Jesus had a very close friendship because John received Jesus' love, and he loved Jesus in return.

8. *Say:* We see the close friendship between John and Jesus when Jesus was hanging on the cross.

Find and read aloud **John 19:25-27**.
Jesus' mother stood near his cross. So did his mother's sister, Mary the wife of Clopas, and Mary Magdalene. Jesus saw his mother there. He also saw the disciple he loved standing nearby.
Jesus said to his mother, "Dear woman, here is your son." He said to the disciple, "Here is your mother." From that time on, the disciple took her into his home.

Say: Jesus wanted His mother to be cared for by John. Jesus knew that John would be able to love her the way He did. Because John was able to receive Jesus' love for him, he was able to love others with great love.

> A lesson we can learn from John's life is: **THE MORE WE ARE OPEN TO RECEIVING JESUS' LOVE FOR US, THE MORE WE WILL BE ABLE TO LOVE OTHER PEOPLE.**

9. *Say:* **NOW LET'S LOOK AT MARY MAGDALENE**, who was the other person to go to Jesus' empty tomb.

Find and read aloud **Luke 8:1-2**.
"After this, Jesus traveled around from one town and village to another. He announced the good news of God's kingdom. His 12 disciples were with him. So were some women who had been healed of evil spirits and sicknesses. One was Mary Magdalene. Seven demons had come out of her."

Ask: How would you feel about Jesus if He freed you from seven evil spirits?
[You would be really grateful and love Him for it! That is how Mary felt. She and other women gave their own money to help buy food for Jesus and the twelve disciples (**Luke 8:3**).]

10. *Find and read aloud* **John 20:11-13**.
But Mary stood outside the tomb crying. As she cried, she bent over to look into the tomb. She saw two angels dressed in white. They were seated where Jesus' body had

been. One of them was where Jesus' head had been laid. The other sat where his feet had been placed.

They asked her, "Woman, why are you crying?"

"They have taken my Lord away," she said. "I don't know where they have put him."

All three, Peter, John and Mary, did not understand what happened to Jesus' body. But Mary was the only one who stayed at the empty tomb. Mary really wanted to find out where Jesus' body had gone. She had loved Jesus, and she wanted to make sure that Jesus' body was cared for. She had a servant's heart, and she was ready to serve Jesus even in death. She had perseverance, which means she stuck with a job until it was done. Because she persevered in looking for Jesus, Mary got the chance to see angels. What a reward!

11. *Find and read aloud* **John 20:14-15.**

Then she turned around and saw Jesus standing there. But she didn't realize that it was Jesus.

He asked her, "Woman, why are you crying? Who are you looking for?"

She thought he was the gardener. So she said, "Sir, did you carry him away? Tell me where you put him. Then I will go and get him."

Ask: Do you think that Mary would be able to carry a dead body all by herself?

[She probably couldn't, but she was willing to try. She was so thankful to Jesus for what He had done for her!]

12. *Find and read aloud* **John 20:16-18:**

Jesus said to her, "Mary."

She turned toward him. Then she cried out in the Aramaic language, "***Rabboni***!" Rabboni means Teacher.

Jesus said, "Do not hold on to me. I have not yet ascended to the Father. Instead, go to those who believe in me. Tell them, 'I am ascending to my Father and your Father, to my God and your God.'"

Mary Magdalene went to the disciples with the news. She said, "I have seen the Lord!" And she told them that he had said these things to her.

Say: Again, Mary was rewarded for her perseverance. She was the first person to see Jesus after He rose from the dead! For some reason, Jesus didn't let Mary recognize Him at first. Notice that she finally recognized Jesus when He called her by name.

Remember, in **John 10:3** Jesus said, **"The sheep listen to his voice. He calls his own sheep by name and leads them out."**

A lesson we can learn from Mary's life is: **IF WE PERSEVERE IN SEEKING GOD, HE IS PLEASED AND WILL HELP US TO KNOW HIM BETTER.**

Say: In **verse 17** Jesus told her "...*Go* to those who believe in me. *Tell* them, 'I am ascending to my Father and your Father, to my God and your God.'" What a message Mary had to share! Jesus gave her the honor of being the first one to share the good news. Jesus was alive! He had risen from the dead, which proved that He was who He said He was—the Son of God.

Jesus sent His followers to share the good news with the help of the Holy Spirit.

1. *Find and read aloud* John 20:19-22.

> On the evening of that first day of the week, the disciples were together. They had locked the doors because they were afraid of the Jewish leaders. Jesus came in and stood among them. He said, "May peace be with you!" Then he showed them his hands and his side. The disciples were very happy when they saw the Lord.
>
> Again Jesus said, "May peace be with you! The Father has sent me. So now I am sending you." He then breathed on them. He said, "Receive the Holy Spirit. If you forgive anyone's sins, their sins are forgiven. If you do not forgive them, they are not forgiven."

Ask: Why do you think that Jesus said **"May peace be with you!"** two times?
[He didn't want them to be afraid. He wanted to give them His peace.]

Say: Finally, the other disciples saw for themselves that Mary was right. Jesus was alive, and He was sending them to go preach the good news.

Jesus breathed on them just as God had breathed life into Adam at creation. When Jesus breathed on them and said, **"Receive the Holy Spirit,"** their spirits were filled with God's life (*zoe*), and they were born again. Although they already believed that Jesus was the Son of God, they could not be born again until after Jesus had died. He had to be raised from the dead and to offer His blood to pay for our sin (**Hebrews 10:10**).

2. *Say*: About 40 days later, Jesus returned to heaven and asked God the Father to send the Holy Spirit to be with His friends forever (**John 14:16, 26**). Jesus' followers prayed and waited until the Holy Spirit came on them and gave them power from God. They told people that Jesus died for them and they needed to repent. That day, more than 3,000 people believed in Jesus and were baptized (**Acts 2:1-4, 41**)! The Lord does not send us to tell people about Jesus without help. We also need the Holy Spirit in order to share the good news and make disciples of Jesus. He will tell us who to talk to and what to say.

3. *Say*: Remember these things so that you can hear God clearly:
   - Obey the Lord and live a life that pleases Him.
   - When you disobey, confess your sin quickly and turn away from that sin.
   - See God as a loving Father, who wants to speak to you.
   - When you ask God a question, get ready to hear Him, and let Him decide how and when to speak to you.

LA #2, AP #2

PRAYER AND MINISTRY TIME

Spend time together praying for friends and family members who don't know Jesus yet. Pray for the children to become fishers of people. Ask the Lord to give them ears to hear God's voice. Pray for boldness, God's love, power and protection as the children go out to share the good news.

LEARNING ACTIVITIES

Activity #1 Feature a missionary.

MATERIALS NEEDED: Paper, envelope, postage stamps, pencil, crayons or markers

Tell the children about someone who is working as a missionary now. Have them write letters or draw pictures for the missionary, to encourage him. Or send letters and pictures for the people the missionary works with, to tell them about Jesus.

Activity #2 Be ready to share the good news.

Have the children ask God what to say to a friend who doesn't know Jesus yet. Have them write out what their friend needs to know about Jesus. Help them practice saying what they wrote. Young children could dictate to you what they want to say about Jesus. Then encourage them to be ready to share the good news with that person when God gives them the "green light."

ART PROJECTS

Project #1 Make a fish badge or necklace.

MATERIALS NEEDED: Construction paper, scissors, markers, safety pin, glue gun, hole punch, ribbon or yarn

Say: The fish shape reminds us that we are followers of Jesus and we get to be "fishers of people."

Have the children trace the Lesson 13 fish pattern on colored construction paper and cut it out. Have each child print his name on it. Help them glue a safety pin on the back with a glue gun to make a fish-shaped badge for your child to wear. Another option would be to use a hole punch and ribbon or yarn to make a fish necklace to wear.

Project #2 Make a "Wordless Book."

MATERIALS NEEDED: Cardstock for the covers, copy paper for the interior pages, three hole punch, yarn or brads, markers, crayons or coloring pencils

Tell the children that they can use this book to tell other people about Jesus. Have them draw pictures that show what they want to say about Jesus. Some picture ideas might be:
- Jesus letting children sit on His lap, to show how much He loves children.
- Jesus helping Peter pull in a net full of fish, to show He can do miracles.
- Jesus healing a lame man, to show that He wants to heal people.
- Jesus on the cross telling John to take care of His mother, Mary. This reminds us to accept Jesus' love for us so that we can love other people well.
- Mary Magdalene kneeling before Jesus at the empty tomb after He was raised from the dead. This reminds us that God rewards us when we seek Him with all of our heart.
- Jesus breathing on the disciples and saying, "Receive the Holy Spirit." This reminds us that we receive the Holy Spirit when we are born again.
- Other pictures that say something about Jesus.

Three-hole punch the covers and picture pages, and hold them together with brads or yarn.

ENDNOTES

Unless otherwise indicated all Scripture quotes come from the *NIrV Adventure Bible for Early Readers Version.*

Lesson 2

1. [hear] Joseph H. Thayer, D.D, *Thayer's Greek-English Lexicon of the New Testament* (Peabody, Massachusetts: Hendrickson Publishers, Inc., 2000), p. 23, #191.

2. [men-ah] Paul Lee Tan, Th.D., *The Encyclopedia of 7700 Illustrations* (Dallas, Texas: Bible Communications, 1979), p. 499, #1961.

3. [excerpt from book] Steve Lightle, *Exodus II—Let My People Go* (Kingwood, Texas: Hunter Books, 1983), pp. 33–35.

Lesson 4

1. [Jared] Finis Jennings Dake, Dake's Annotated Reference Bible (Lawrenceville, Georgia: Dake Bible Sales, Inc., 1963), p. 5, column 4, note b.

2. [Enoch] Ibid., note d.

3. [Methuselah] Ibid., note e.

4. [Lamech] Ibid., notes i and n.

5. [Noah] Ibid., note k.

6. [raven] The Encyclopedia Americana, Vol. 23 (Danbury, Connecticut: Grolier, Inc., 1993), p. 274.

7. [dove/seeds] The Encyclopedia Americana, Vol. 9 (1993), p. 316.

Lesson 5

1. [spirit, soul, body] Charles R. Solomon, *Handbook to Happiness* (Wheaton, Illinois: Tyndale Publishers, 1989), p. 26.

2. [sarx] James Strong, LL.D., S.T.D., *Strong's Exhaustive Concordance of the Bible* (Nashville, Tennessee: Thomas Nelson Publishers), #4561.

3. [psuche] Ibid., #5590 and William Morris, Ed., *The American Heritage Dictionary of the English Language* (Boston, Massachusetts: American Heritage Publishing Co., Inc. and Houghton Mifflin Company, 1969), p. 1181.

4. [pneuma] Strong, #4151 within #5590.

5. [kardia] Allen C. Myers, Ed., *The Eerdmans Bible Dictionary* (Grand Rapids, Michigan: William B. Eerdmans Publishing Company, 1987), p. 471.

Lesson 9

1. [go ahead] Kenneth Hagin, *How You Can Be Led By The Spirit Of God* (Tulsa, Oklahoma: RHEMA Bible Church AKA Kenneth Hagin Ministries, 1991), p. 25.

2. [uneasiness] Ibid., p. 24.

3. [inner knowing] Ibid., p. 27.

4. [wait] Ibid., p. 34.

Lesson 11

1. [Samuel's age] *The NIV Study Bible* (Grand Rapids, Michigan: Zondervan Publishing House, 1985), p. 379, footnote 3:1.

Lesson 12

1. [word of knowledge] Dick Iverson, *The Holy Spirit Today* (Portland, Oregon: Bible Temple Publishing, 1987), pp. 114-115.

2. [word of wisdom] Ibid., p. 104.

SALVATION SCRIPTURES

SALVATION SCRIPTURES

1. **Preparation for Salvation (being born again)**
   a. John 3:16 NIrV

      "God so loved the world that he gave his one and only Son. Anyone who believes in him will not die but will have eternal life."

   b. Romans 3:23

      "Everyone has sinned. No one measures up to God's glory."

   c. Romans 6:23

      "When you sin, the pay you get is death. But God gives you the gift of eternal life. That's because of what Christ Jesus our Lord has done."

   d. John 1:12-13

      "Some people did accept him and did believe in his name. He gave them the right to become children of God. To be a child of God has nothing to do with human parents. Children of God are not born because of human choice or because a husband wants them to be born. They are born because of what God does."

   e. John 7:37-39

      "It was the last and most important day of the feast. Jesus stood up and spoke in a loud voice. He said, 'Let anyone who is thirsty come to me and drink. Does anyone believe in me? Then, just as Scripture says, rivers of living water will flow from inside them.' When he said this, he meant the Holy Spirit. Those who believed in Jesus would receive the Spirit later. Up to that time, the Spirit had not been given. This was because Jesus had not yet received glory."

2. **Confession/Prayer**
   Romans 10:9-11

   "Say with your mouth, 'Jesus is Lord.' Believe in your heart that God raised him from the dead. Then you will be saved. With your heart you believe and are made right with God. With your mouth you say what you believe. And so you are saved. Scripture says, 'The one who believes in him will never be put to shame.'"

3. **What Has Happened?**
   a. Romans 10:13

      "Scripture says, 'Everyone who calls on the name of the Lord will be saved.'"

   b. Ezekiel 36:26-27

      "I will give you new hearts. I will give you a new spirit that is faithful to me. I will remove your stubborn hearts from you. I will give you hearts that obey me. I will put my Spirit in you. I will make you want to obey my rules. I want you to be careful to keep my laws."

4. **Follow-Up**
   a. Read the book of John to learn more about Jesus and the new relationship you have with Him.
   b. Talk with mature Christians and ask any questions you have. Go with them to church.

RECOMMENDED READING

I Was Wrong, but God Made Me Right! by Frank Friedmann

This short booklet explains to children, in terms and pictures they can understand, the Good News of salvation and life in God through Jesus Christ. Find online at Store—Living in Grace—frankfriedmann.org/resources/, then choose Store—Living in Grace.

Hearing God Through Your Dreams: Understanding the Language God Speaks at Night by Mark Virkler and Charity Virkler Kayembe (Destiny Image Publishers: Shippensburg, Pennsylvania, 2016).

This book contains a chapter on children's dreams. Chapter 11 gives guidance on knowing if a dream your child has had is from God with a message or whether it is a dream that the brain naturally uses to sort out feelings about daytime events. Parents are helped to know how to speak to their children about their dreams and how to discern what God is saying to them.

SUGGESTED MATERIALS LIST

For Lesson 1 Activities and Projects
- A phone or computer connected to the internet
- A large bowl, colander, knives, several different kinds of fruit
- Construction paper, scissors, markers or crayons, safety pins, hot glue gun, Lesson 1 ribbon pattern
- Crayons, markers or colored pencils

For Lesson 2 Activities and Projects
- Cardboard, construction paper and clothes, OR cardboard, scissors, string and markers
- Construction paper and scissors, Lesson 2 story field patterns
- A Bible
- Branches, cardboard boxes or other material to create a sheepfold
- A phone or computer with internet access
- A glass jar, water, iodine and dropper, hydrogen peroxide, tablespoon measuring spoon, a spoon
- Crayons, markers or colored pencils

For Lesson 3 Activities and Projects
- A blindfold and a telephone that can send and receive text messages
- A computer or telephone that has internet access
- A blindfold and large objects for an obstacle course
- Markers, crayons or colored pencils

For Lesson 4 Activities and Projects
- Tag board, masking tape, yardstick and scissors
- A set of crayons, coloring pencils or markers for the leader and each player, copies of the Lesson 4 Noah's ark coloring page
- A computer or telephone that has internet access
- Red and green construction paper, a popsicle stick and glue, Lesson 4 circle pattern OR Red, green and white construction paper, a paint stirring stick, crayons, glue and Lesson 4 circle pattern
- Butcher paper, pencils and markers
- A wire hanger or two wooden dowels tied together in a cross, string, Lesson 4 mobile patterns, scissors, crayons or markers and stapler
- Watercolor paper, watercolors, brushes, jars of water and paper towels

For Lesson 5 Activities and Projects
- Tall clear glass, spoon, milk, chocolate syrup and a plate
- Three colors of play-dough, gingerbread man cookie cutter
- Three colors of sidewalk chalk
- Lesson 5 body, spirit and soul patterns, paper, scissors, glue, crayons or pencils

For Lesson 6 Activities and Projects
- Butcher block paper, crayons or magic markers
- Gingerbread dough—either pre-made or from scratch, gingerbread man cookie cutter, icing with a nozzle, candy heart or chocolate chip.
- A phone or computer with internet access
- Markers, crayons or colored pencils

For Lesson 7 Activities and Projects
- King's crown, soldier's swords, musical instruments, a computer or telephone that has internet access, or a recording of a praise song that describes God's goodness and power
- A Bible
- Markers, crayons or colored pencils
- An oatmeal container, wrapping paper, scissors and glue
- Plastic or paper cup, hammer and nail, yarn, Scotch tape, scissors and jingle bells
- Two aluminum pie pans, jingle bells, colorful electrical tape, colorful fabric and scissors

For Lesson 8 Activities and Projects
- A phone or computer with internet access
- Plastic knives, ingredients for chocolate cake cupcakes and liners, or chocolate graham crackers, ingredients for frosting, OR dark bread, cream cheese
- The board game Chutes and Ladders
- Lesson 8 crown pattern, gold construction paper, crayons, scissors, "jewel" stickers, stapler or tape

For Lesson 9 Activities and Projects
- A blindfold
- A stretchy, resistance band
- Lesson 4 circle pattern, red and green construction paper, a popsicle stick and glue, OR Lesson 4 circle pattern, red, green and white construction paper, a paint stirring stick, crayons, and glue

For Lesson 10 Activities and Projects
- A child or an object to hide
- A Sound Bingo Game set
- OR Two 8 ½ x 11-inch pieces of card stock, scissors, ruler, pencil, colored markers, copies of the Lesson 10 sound pictures, glue, tokens (e.g. pennies, poker chips, dried pasta or Cheerios), 12 index cards, pen or pencil, a bottle of water, glass, pencil with an eraser and paper, a piece of paper to rip, hard cover book, two dice, pen that clicks, Scotch tape dispenser, pepper grinder, cracker
- Paper, scissors, pen or pencil
- A plate, sliced bread, peanut butter, jelly, a knife
- Card stock, ruler, scissors, a hole punch, ribbon or yarn, markers or crayons

For Lesson 11 Activities and Projects
- A tape recorder or recording application on a smart phone
- A blindfold and a treat to eat
- Vanilla and chocolate sandwich cookies, OR vanilla and chocolate pudding
- A Bible
- A phone or computer with internet access
- Lesson 11 Samuel coloring picture, crayons, black tempera paint, brushes
- Colored pencils

For Lesson 12 Activities and Projects
- A phone or computer with internet access
- A Bible
- Clay or play-dough, paper, watercolors, brushes, markers, colored pencils, magazine pages, scissors, glue, cardboard, Scotch tape
- Paper, marker, crayons or paint and brushes

For Lesson 13 Activities and Projects

- Two 8 ½ x 11-inch pieces of card stock, copy paper, three hole punch, yarn or brads, markers, crayons or coloring pencils
- Paper, envelope, postage stamps, pencil, crayons or markers
- Lesson 13 fish pattern, construction paper, scissors, markers, safety pin, hot glue gun, hole punch, ribbon or yarn